FRANCIS FRITH'S

TEST VALLEY

PHOTOGRAPHIC MEMORIES

DAVID ALLEN is Senior Keeper of Archaeology with the Hampshire County Council Museums & Archives Service. For more than twenty years he was curator at the museum in Andover and had ample opportunity to explore the history and natural beauty of the Test Valley, north and south. This is his second book for The Francis Frith Collection, and he dedicates it to D, D, B and T who have been a constant source of encouragement to all his literary efforts.

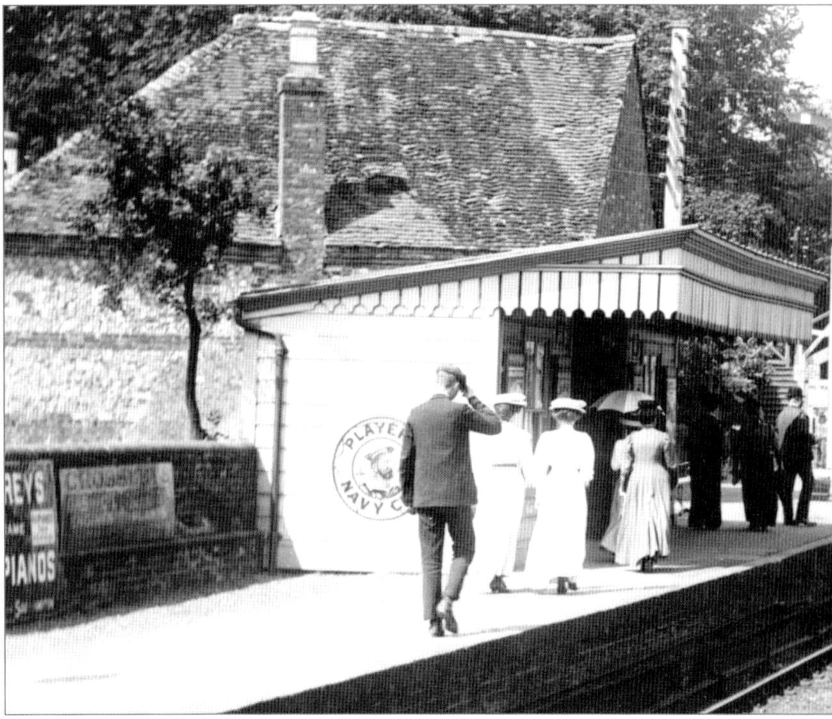

FRANCIS FRITH'S
PHOTOGRAPHIC MEMORIES

TEST VALLEY

PHOTOGRAPHIC MEMORIES

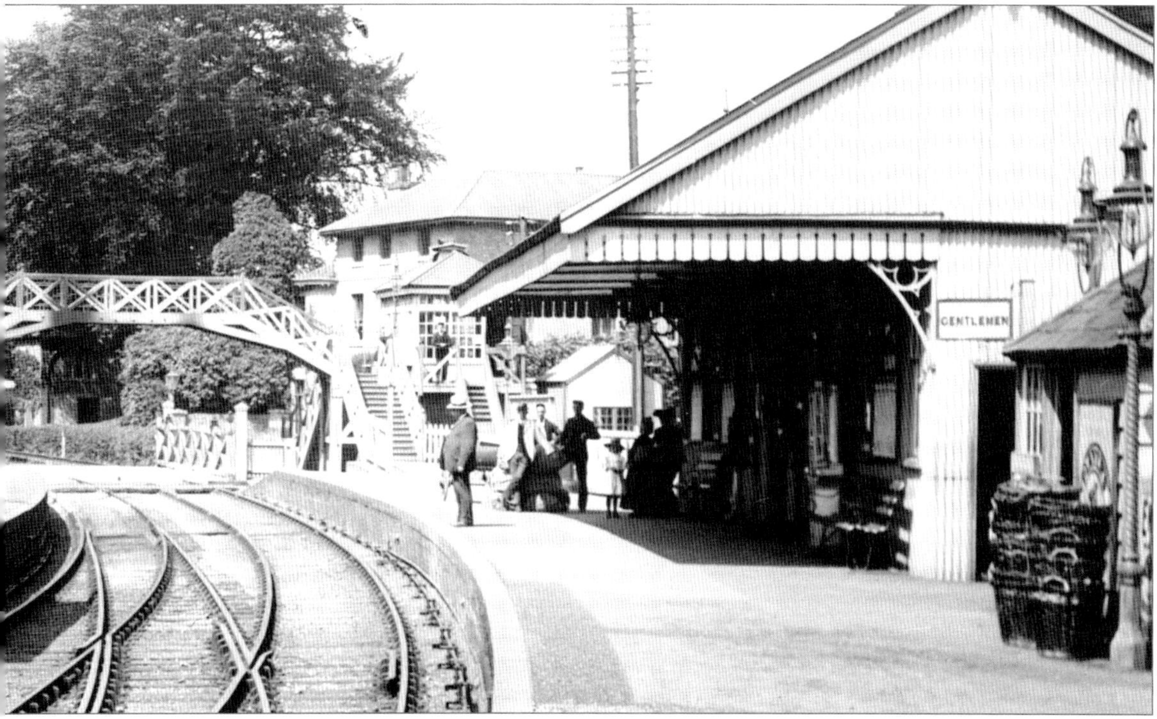

DAVID ALLEN

THE FRANCIS FRITH COLLECTION

First published in paperback in the United Kingdom in 2011 by
The Francis Frith Collection®

ISBN: 978-1-5937-973-8

British Library Cataloguing in Publication Data

Test Valley Photographic Memories
David Allen

The Francis Frith Collection®
Unit 6, Oakley Business Park,
Wylye Road, Dinton,
Wiltshire SP3 5EU
Tel: +44 (0) 1722 716 376
Email: info@francisfrith.co.uk
www.francisfrith.com

Printed and bound in Great Britain

Front Cover: **CHILBOLTON,** *Testcombe, The Seven Stars c1907* C227301t
Frontispiece: **ANDOVER**, *Town Station 1908* 60096

The colour-tinting is for illustrative purposes only, and is not intended to be historically accurate

AS WITH ANY HISTORICAL DATABASE THE FRITH ARCHIVE IS CONSTANTLY BEING CORRECTED AND IMPROVED AND THE PUBLISHERS WOULD WELCOME INFORMATION ON OMISSIONS OR INACCURACIES

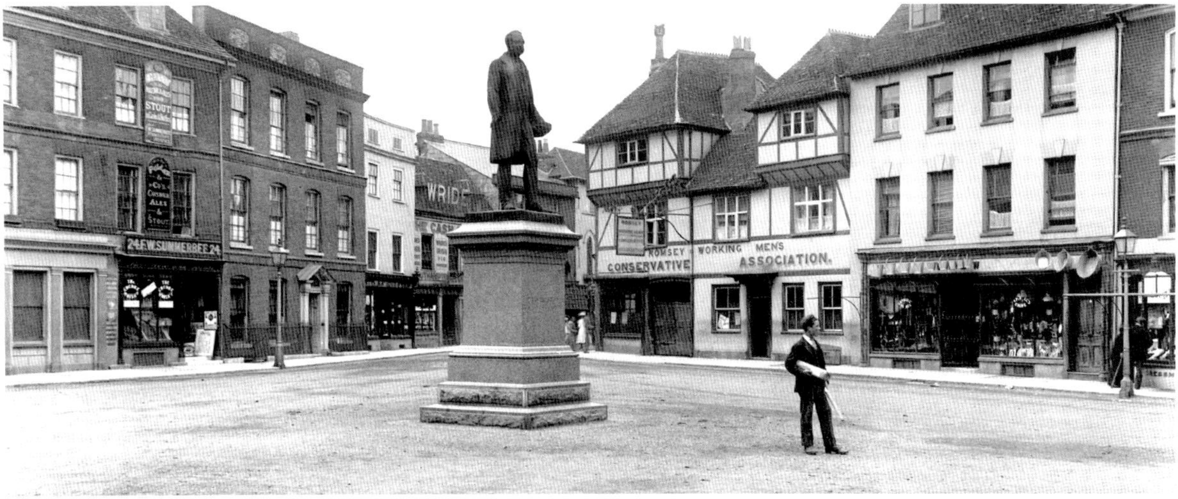
STOUT
ALES
STOUT
24 F.W. SUMMERBEE 24
WRIDE
ROMSEY WORKING MENS
CONSERVATIVE ASSOCIATION

CONTENTS

FRANCIS FRITH
VICTORIAN PIONEER

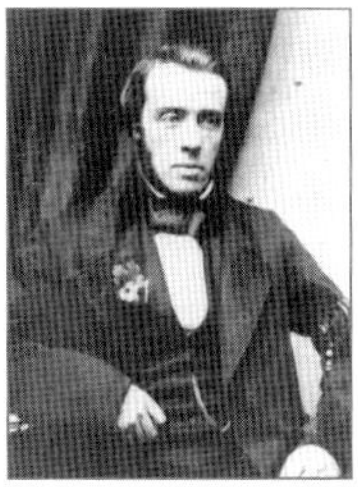

FRANCIS FRITH, founder of the world-famous photographic archive, was a complex and multi-talented man. A devout Quaker and a highly successful Victorian businessman, he was philosophical by nature and pioneering in outlook.

By 1855 he had already established a wholesale grocery business in Liverpool, and sold it for the astonishing sum of £200,000, which is the equivalent today of over £15,000,000. Now a very rich man, he was able to indulge his passion for travel. As a child he had pored over travel books written by early explorers, and his fancy and imagination had been stirred by family holidays to the sublime mountain regions of Wales and Scotland. 'What lands of spirit-stirring and enriching scenes and places!' he had written. He was to return to these scenes of grandeur in later years to 'recapture the thousands of vivid and tender memories', but with a different purpose. Now in his thirties, and captivated by the new science of photography, Frith set out on a series of pioneering journeys up the Nile and to the Near East that occupied him from 1856 until 1860.

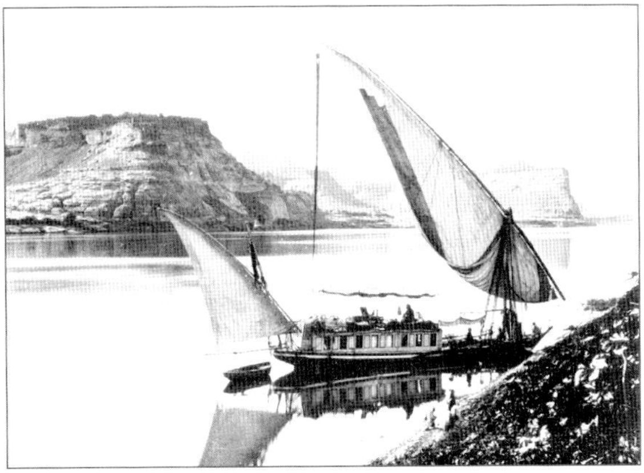

INTRIGUE AND EXPLORATION

These far-flung journeys were packed with intrigue and adventure. In his life story, written when he was sixty-three, Frith tells of being held captive by bandits, and of fighting 'an awful midnight battle to the very point of surrender with a deadly pack of hungry, wild dogs'. Wearing flowing Arab costume, Frith arrived at Akaba by camel sixty years before Lawrence of Arabia, where he encountered 'desert princes and rival sheikhs, blazing with jewel-hilted swords'.

He was the first photographer to venture beyond the sixth cataract of the Nile. Africa was still the mysterious 'Dark Continent', and Stanley and Livingstone's historic meeting was a decade into the future. The conditions for picture taking confound belief. He laboured for hours in his wicker dark-room in the sweltering heat of the desert, while the volatile chemicals fizzed dangerously in their trays. Back in London he exhibited his photographs and was 'rapturously cheered' by members of the Royal Society. His reputation as a photographer was made overnight.

VENTURE OF A LIFE-TIME

Characteristically, Frith quickly spotted the opportunity to create a new business as a specialist publisher of photographs. He lived in an era of immense and sometimes violent change.

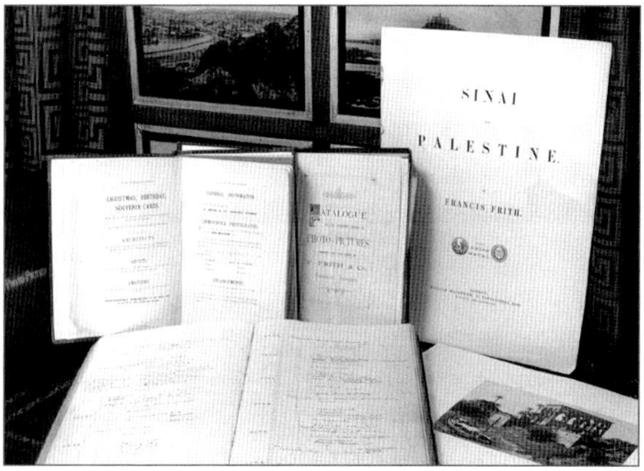

For the poor in the early part of Victoria's reign work was exhausting and the hours long, and people had precious little free time to enjoy themselves. Most had no transport other than a cart or gig at their disposal, and rarely travelled far beyond the boundaries of their own town or village. However, by the 1870s the railways had threaded their way across the country, and Bank Holidays and half-day Saturdays had been made obligatory by Act of Parliament. All of a sudden the working man and his family were able to enjoy days out and see a little more of the world.

With typical business acumen, Francis Frith foresaw that these new tourists would enjoy having souvenirs to commemorate their days out. In 1860 he married Mary Ann Rosling and set out on a new career: his aim was to photograph every city, town and village in Britain. For the next thirty years he travelled the country by train and by pony and trap, producing fine photographs of seaside resorts and beauty spots that were keenly bought by millions of Victorians. These prints were painstakingly pasted into family albums and pored over during the dark nights of winter, rekindling precious memories of summer excursions.

THE RISE OF FRITH & CO

Frith's studio was soon supplying retail shops all over the country. To meet the demand he gathered about him a small team of photographers, and published the work of independent artist-photographers of the calibre of Roger Fenton and Francis Bedford. In order to gain some understanding of the scale of Frith's business one only has to look at the catalogue issued by Frith & Co in 1886: it runs to some 670 pages, listing not only many thousands of views of the British Isles but also many photographs of most European countries, and China, Japan, the USA and Canada - note the sample page shown on page 9 from the hand-written Frith & Co ledgers recording the pictures. By 1890 Frith had created the greatest specialist photographic publishing company in the world, with over 2,000 sales outlets - more than the combined number that Boots and WH Smith have today! The picture on the next page shows the Frith & Co display board at Ingleton in the Yorkshire Dales (left of window). Beautifully constructed with a mahogany frame and gilt inserts, it could display up to a dozen local scenes.

POSTCARD BONANZA

The ever-popular holiday postcard we know today took many years to develop. In 1870 the Post Office issued the first plain cards, with a pre-printed stamp on one face. In 1894 they allowed other publishers' cards to be sent through the mail with an attached adhesive halfpenny stamp. Demand grew rapidly, and in 1895 a new size of postcard was permitted called the court card, but there was little room for illustration. In 1899, a year after Frith's death, a new card measuring 5.5 x 3.5 inches became the standard format, but it was not until 1902 that the divided back came into being, so that the address and message could be on one face and a full-size illustration on the other. Frith & Co were in the vanguard of postcard development: Frith's sons Eustace and Cyril continued their father's monumental task, expanding the number of views offered to the public and recording more and more places

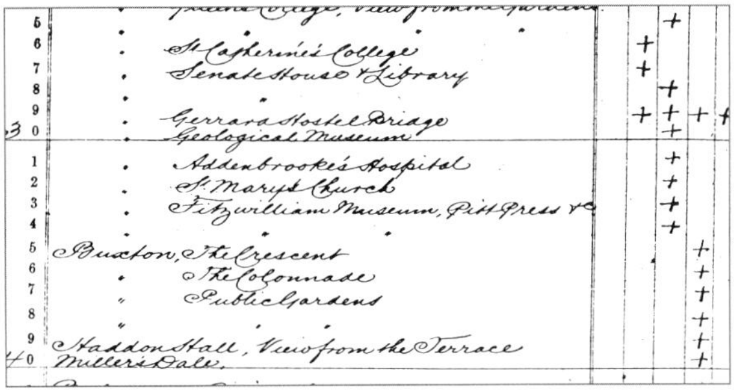

5
6 St Catherine's College
7 Senate House & Library
8
9 Gerrard Hostel Bridge
30 Geological Museum
1 Addenbrooke's Hospital
2 St Mary's Church
3 Fitzwilliam Museum, Pitt Press &c
4
5 Buxton, The Crescent
6 The Colonnade
7 Public Gardens
8
9 Haddon Hall, View from the Terrace
40 Miller's Dale

in Britain, as the coasts and countryside were opened up to mass travel.

Francis Frith had died in 1898 at his villa in Cannes, his great project still growing. The archive he created continued in business for another seventy years. By 1970 it contained over a third of a million pictures showing 7,000 British towns and villages.

FRANCIS FRITH'S LEGACY

Frith's legacy to us today is of immense significance and value, for the magnificent archive of evocative photographs he created provides a unique record of change in the cities, towns and villages throughout Britain over a century and more. Frith and his fellow studio photographers revisited locations many times down the years to update their views, compiling for us an enthralling and colourful pageant of British life and character.

We are fortunate that Frith was dedicated to recording the minutiae of everyday life, for it is this sheer wealth of visual data, the painstaking chronicle of changes in dress, transport, street layouts, buildings, housing, engineering and landscape that captivates us so much today. His remarkable images offer us a powerful link with the past and with the lives of our ancestors.

THE VALUE OF THE ARCHIVE TODAY

Computers have now made it possible for Frith's many thousands of images to be accessed almost instantly. Frith's images are increasingly used as visual resources, by social historians, by researchers into genealogy and ancestry, by architects and town planners, and by teachers involved in local history projects.

In addition, the archive offers every one of us an opportunity to examine the places where we and our families have lived and worked down the years. Highly successful in Frith's own era, the archive is now, a century and more on, entering a new phase of popularity. Historians consider the Francis Frith Collection to be of prime national importance. It is the only archive of its kind remaining in private ownership. Francis Frith's archive is now housed in an historic timber barn in the beautiful village of Teffont in Wiltshire. Its founder would not recognize the archive office as it is today. In place of the many thousands of dusty boxes containing glass plate negatives and an all-pervading odour of photographic chemicals, there are now ranks of computer screens. He would be amazed to watch his images travelling round the world at unimaginable speeds through internet lines.

The archive's future is both bright and exciting. Francis Frith, with his unshakeable belief in making photographs available to the greatest number of people, would undoubtedly approve of what is being done today with his lifetime's work. His photographs depicting our shared past are now bringing pleasure and enlightenment to millions around the world a century and more after his death.

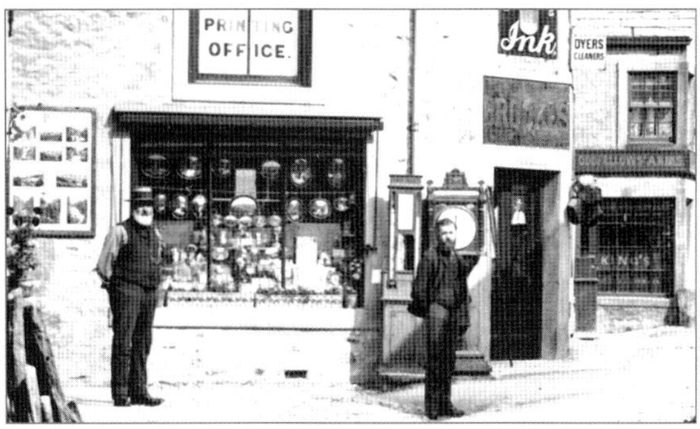

TEST VALLEY
AN INTRODUCTION

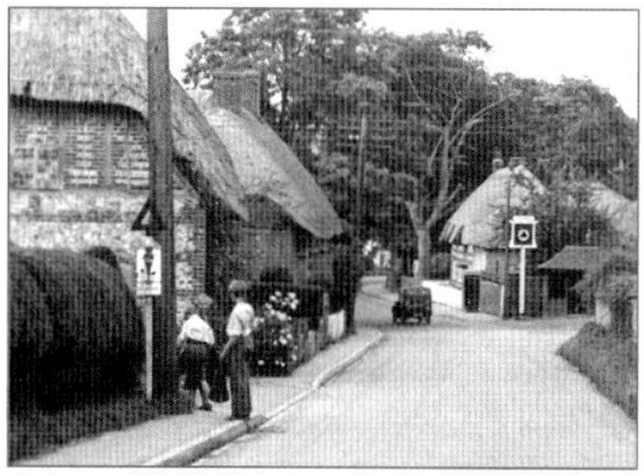

ANDOVER AND ROMSEY, standing at either end of the local government district of Test Valley, apparently have little in common. Romsey, with its imposing Norman abbey and a market place presided over by a brooding Lord Palmerston (whose forebears forged a lasting link between the town and nearby Broadlands), is quite different in character from Andover. Here the abiding image is of housing and industrial estates - initially born of an agreement struck forty years ago with the Greater London Council - crowding in on its historic core.

This distinction has been emphasised by other 20th-century developments. Andover and Romsey stand on a north-south axis, but the main grain of transport links, for example the A303, the M27, and the surviving railways, is east-west, ignoring the true lie of the land. Long gone are the days when the 'Sprat and Winkle' railway, itself replacing an earlier if unprofitable canal, carried the unhurried passenger between the two centres. In addition, the proximity to Salisbury Plain made Andover something of a garrison town, serving the needs of a large military population in peace and war.

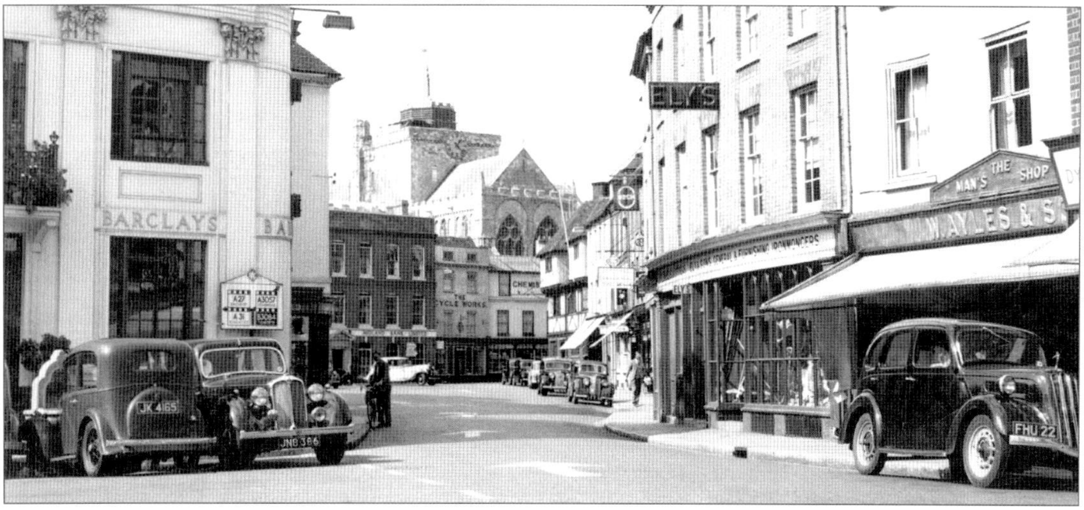

ROMSEY, *The Market Place c1955* R53019

Despite these divergent strands the two towns share a great deal, not just in their early history, but also in more recent times. Clearly the most significant unifying feature is the River Test and its tributaries, such as the Bourne, the Anton, the Pillhill and the Wallop brooks, the Somborne stream, and the River Dun. It is these, in this selection of images, which are never far from the photographer's lens.

The Test Valley is full of evidence for prehistoric and Romano-British settlement, but it is with the Saxons that the two towns and many of the villages were founded. The new settlers were drawn towards previously ignored or under-exploited stream and riverside locations, and they bestowed many of the place-names that have survived to the present day. Romsey, a permanent settlement from about AD700, and the site of a nunnery 200 years later, means 'Rum's island', Rum being an influential Saxon who lived in the late 10th century. Andover, a royal estate close to hunting forests, was simply named after its river, 'Onnadubri', or 'river of the ash trees', and this too is first recorded in the late 10th century. Known today as the Anton, the river flows into the Test at Fullerton.

At Wherwell ('cauldron' or 'bubbling streams' - another late Saxon name), another nunnery was founded in AD986. Under the guiding hand of the Abbess Euphemia it made good use of the watercourses to maintain healthy conditions at what was, until the Dissolution, a devout community. Somborne, as in Kings Somborne, means 'pig stream', and Hurstbourne, as in Hurstbourne Tarrant, may mean 'tendril stream' in relation to some unspecified water plant. At the Clatfords, the plant is mentioned - the name means 'ford where the burdock grows'. Wallop is a more difficult name to interpret, but it may describe a 'hidden valley'. These few examples show the influence of topography on the names of Test Valley settlements, and the importance of the river system in that landscape.

The early origin of several sites is also reflected in the fabric of their churches, despite the Victorian penchant for restoring and rebuilding, sometimes to excess. Elements of Norman architecture are known at twelve of the eighteen churches included here, and are far and away the oldest surviving fragments in most locations.

It is, however, the vernacular architecture that is one of the strongest unifying links, north to south. Thatched roofs abound, occurring in nearly half the photographs, reflecting traditional methods of building cottages and barns in locally available materials. Beneath them the occasional cruck or more common timber-framed structure employs chalk cob, wattle and daub, wood, or flint and brick infilling set on flint foundations, or the walls can be built from banded brick and flint throughout. It is not surprising that these dwellings and outbuildings, representing a centuries-old practice, were so attractive to the photographer. It is gratifying that many of them pictured here survive to this day. Although 'mellowed as completely to their surroundings as their grey churches', they may no longer, in most cases, enjoy 'an air of immemorial quiet and a human life that is part of nature's, unstrenuous, slow and sweet', as described by W H Hudson (1909), but they are still there.

Throughout the valley the most important industry was farming, particularly sheep rearing and corn growing, and the latter is reflected in the number of watermills, perhaps as many as fifty, on the Test and its tributaries. The chalk streams were especially suited to milling as their flow was steady and reliable, and many of the mills are mentioned in Domesday. Two examples are included here, Andover Town Mills and Fullerton.

Also serving the demands of agriculture was Tasker's Ironworks. Robert Tasker first set up in business as a blacksmith in Abbotts Ann in 1809, but within a few years had moved to Anna Valley; here he reclaimed Clatford Marsh by using chalk from an adjacent pit, and harnessed the Pillhill Brook as power for the foundry. As non-conformists and machine makers the Taskers encountered considerable early opposition, but the works grew to cover 11 acres and employ more than 600. Although the foundry has now gone, its legacy remains in the form of bridges, other structural ironwork, and many preserved machines.

One other industry demands attention. In the late 19th century three ailing breweries were bought up by the Faber family and united under the banner of Strong & Co of Romsey Ltd. No doubt Test water was used to good effect at various stages of the brewing process. The remarkable thing is that all the pictured public houses in this book that declare an allegiance, at Sherfield English, Stockbridge, Testcombe and Weyhill, are with Strongs. The Strong empire certainly viewed the Test Valley as a fertile hinterland.

A journey down the Test and its headwaters starts in 'High Hampshire', north of Hurstbourne Tarrant. In this bare chalk country of open landscape with areas of woodland and deep combes the River Swift and the Bourne rivulet meet and head south-east to join the main watercourse. The area around Hurstbourne Tarrant was a favoured destination for William Cobbett during his 'Rural Rides' (1832), and he often sang its praises. 'This to my fancy is a very nice country. It is continual hill and dell ... The undulations are endless, and the great variety in the height, breadth, length and form of the little hills has a very delightful effect.'

When visiting the village 'worth going many miles to see', Cobbett stayed with Joseph Blount,

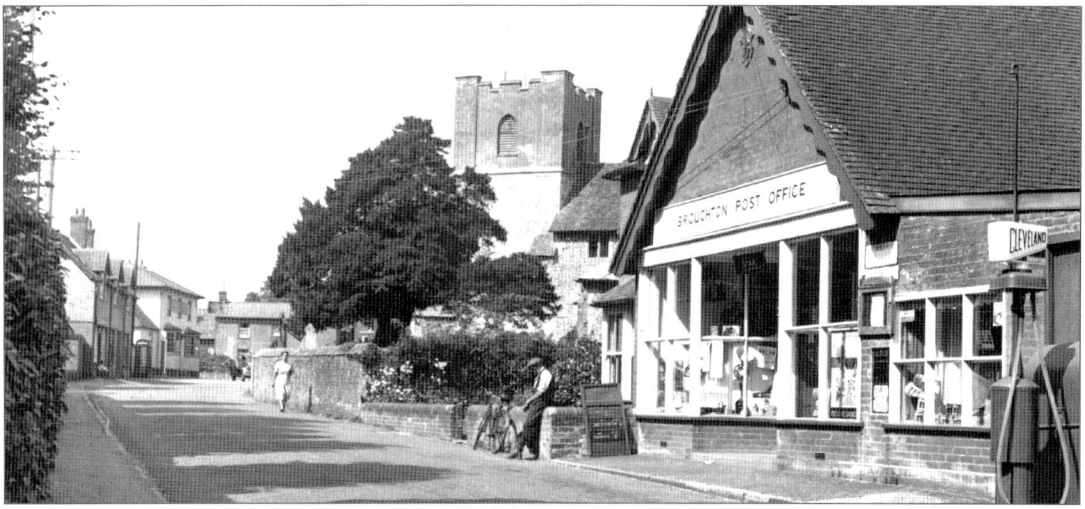

BROUGHTON, *The Post Office and the Church c1955* B897009

perhaps the original 'Joe Blunt', at Rookery Farm. Blount was a true philanthropist who kept 'wayfarers' tables' outside his house piled with potatoes and pickled pork for needy passers-by. He also asked to be buried beneath a large flat grave slab, so that boys could play marbles on it. A later portrait of life at Hurstbourne Tarrant, 'A Hamlet in Old Hampshire' (1902) by the American artist Anna Lea Merritt, depicts the monotony and hardship faced by a rural community of a century ago.

The Bourne, often an occasional stream in its upper reaches, joins the Test at Longparish, and at this point sportsmen extolled the area's virtues. Colonel Peter Hawker of Longparish House kept detailed diaries from 1809 to 1853. In September 1815 he shot 90 partridges, 11 hares, and sundry other species, all in the space of a week. Three years later he estimated his single season's haul of trout from the Test at a ton! He also found time to write a treatise on the pianoforte. A century later his exploits, with the fishing rod at least, were emulated by the celebrated concert singer Harry Plunkett Greene, whose 'Where the Bright Waters Meet' (1924) immortalised this stretch of river.

As the Test braids and broadens past Wherwell and the site of its abbey, and Chilbolton Common with its natural beauty, further tributaries join from east and west. The western streams, feeding into the River Anton, have already given life to Charlton, Andover, Weyhill, Thruxton, Amport, Abbotts Ann, the foundry at Anna Valley and the Clatford villages, before they swell the waters of the main river.

From Weyhill come memories of the famous sheep fair, once the greatest of its kind, and an inspiration to Thomas Hardy in 'The Mayor of Casterbridge'. The fair had its origins in Saxon times, and a court of 'Piepowder' (from the French 'pieds poudreux' - dusty feet) was held there to dispense quick justice to those who travelled there. In the early 20th century the first motorists and long-suffering villagers knew the chalk roads around Weyhill as the dustiest in Hampshire, throwing up the most insidious white powder and coating hedgerows like snow. From Andover comes awareness of a long and colourful past as a market town, overshadowed but not obscured by the recent painful process of change.

But the Test flows on past Longstock, where the ledger stone in the church to the Rev Henry Arnold - 'few equalled, none excelled him' - has been erased, presumably to save the feelings of his successors; from here the river makes for Stockbridge.

Stockbridge was a comparatively late arrival in the Test Valley, being created as a wide chalk causeway providing a valley crossing, as well as a site for occupation and a market, probably under the guidance of William de Briwere in the late 12th century. It was a focus for the old drove roads, and one establishment advertised its benefits in Welsh – many drovers had brought their beasts all the way from Wales. Another inscription, on the old bridge, asked travellers to 'saye of youre charyte a pater noster and an ave for the sowllys' of its founders and makers. More persistent and persuasive demands were made of the population at election time, as Stockbridge was one of the rottenest of 'rotten boroughs'.

In more recent times the pursuit of leisure and pleasure drew people to Stockbridge. The Danebury Races were a famous gathering ground from the 18th to the late 19th century; trainers like the Day family and jockeys like Tom Cannon were innovative and successful, while royalty and nobility got up to the sort of things that royalty and nobility often did. Another celebrated achievement was the founding of the Houghton Fishing Club by Canon Beadon and Edward Barnard in 1822. This is probably the oldest angling club in the world, and its select membership meets in the room above the porch at the Grosvenor Hotel.

The blue green-haired waters of the Test flow on past Stockbridge Marsh and Marsh Court, a much younger country seat than most, until they reach Bossington, where the Wallop Brook, having chattered through the Wallops and Broughton, enters from the west, and the Somborne from the east. It was at Kings Somborne that John of Gaunt (1340-99) had a palace and a deer park, and earthwork traces can be found of both.

By now the Test is the greenest of green valleys, as the waters speed through meadow and marsh and the myriad streams develop into a wide, deep and noble river. At Romsey the waters have inevitably been channelled and tamed and the original 'island' lost to view, but the impassively grey tower of the abbey is just visible above the houses in the Market Square, standing serene as 'paltry neighbours crowd insistently upon it' as D H Moutray Read noted in 'Highways and Byways in Hampshire' (1923). Many consider it the finest conventual church in the south of England, the epitome of the development of our ecclesiastical architecture, and the story of how it was purchased by the town at the Dissolution for £100, an enormous sum in those days, is well known. No other abbey lands were included, however, and the town has had to support the church ever since. In the course of his long ministry (1860-92), the Rev E L Berthon reset the east windows, re-roofed the north transept, and made many other improvements.

The final image in the book is of white-porticoed Broadlands, home of the great Whig statesman the 3rd Viscount Palmerston, who died in Prime Ministerial office in 1865 at the age of 81. Beyond Broadlands, and below Romsey, the Test is no longer a chalk stream; the valley opens out into a broad flood plain receiving numerous small streams, till the river finally empties itself by two channels into the tidal estuary at Redbridge, its journey done.

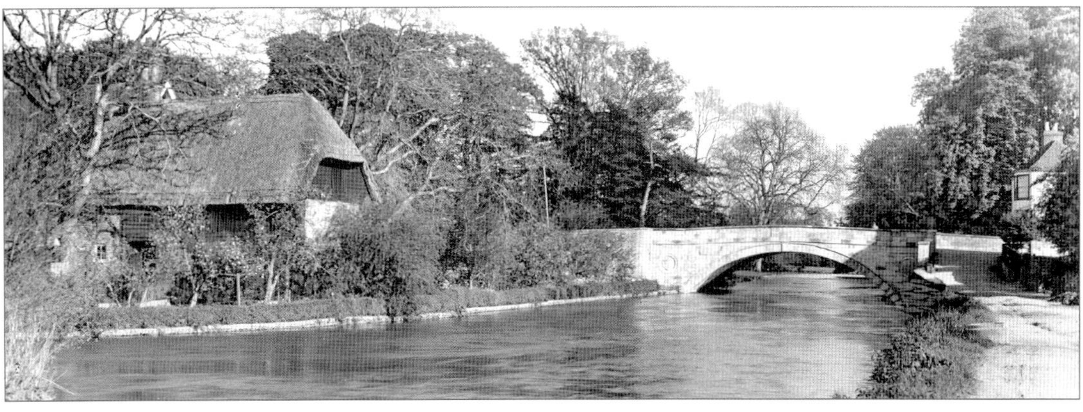

ROMSEY, *Middlebridge and the River Test 1932* 85042

AROUND THE TEST VALLEY

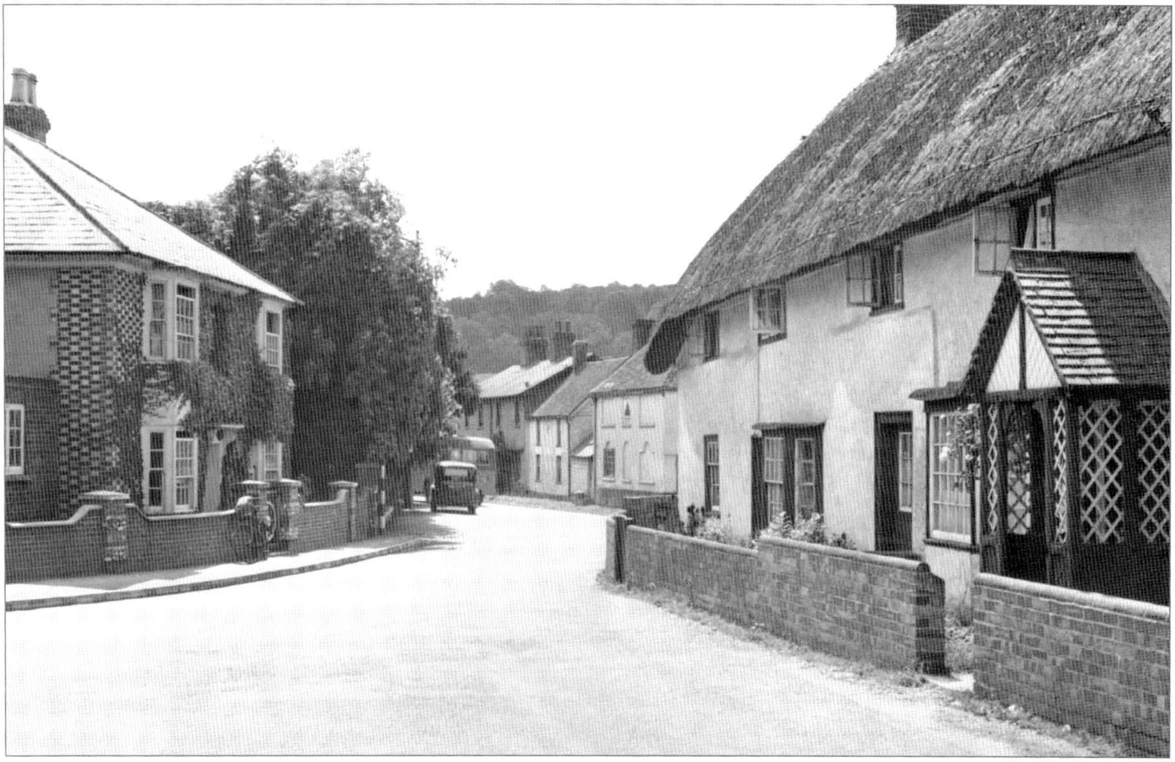

HURSTBOURNE TARRANT, *The Village 1955* H417020

William Cobbett referred to the village by its old name, 'Uphusband'. It is a crossroads village lying along a wide valley with steep chalk hills on either side. This view was taken looking east at the crossroads; the foreground is filled with the two 18th-century cottages of Home Farm, their lime-washed plaster façade masking an earlier timber-framed structure. Just beyond is a glimpse of the George & Dragon, an old coaching inn, and beyond that a modern motor coach negotiates Church Street.

HURSTBOURNE TARRANT
The Village 1955 H417015

As we look west towards the crossroads a real mix of building materials is evident, including flint, brick, timber, thatch, and slate, with styles to match. Behind the car is one of the village shops, promoting the ubiquitous Hovis. Opposite the large white gable wall is Plough House, originally a public house but now dwellings.

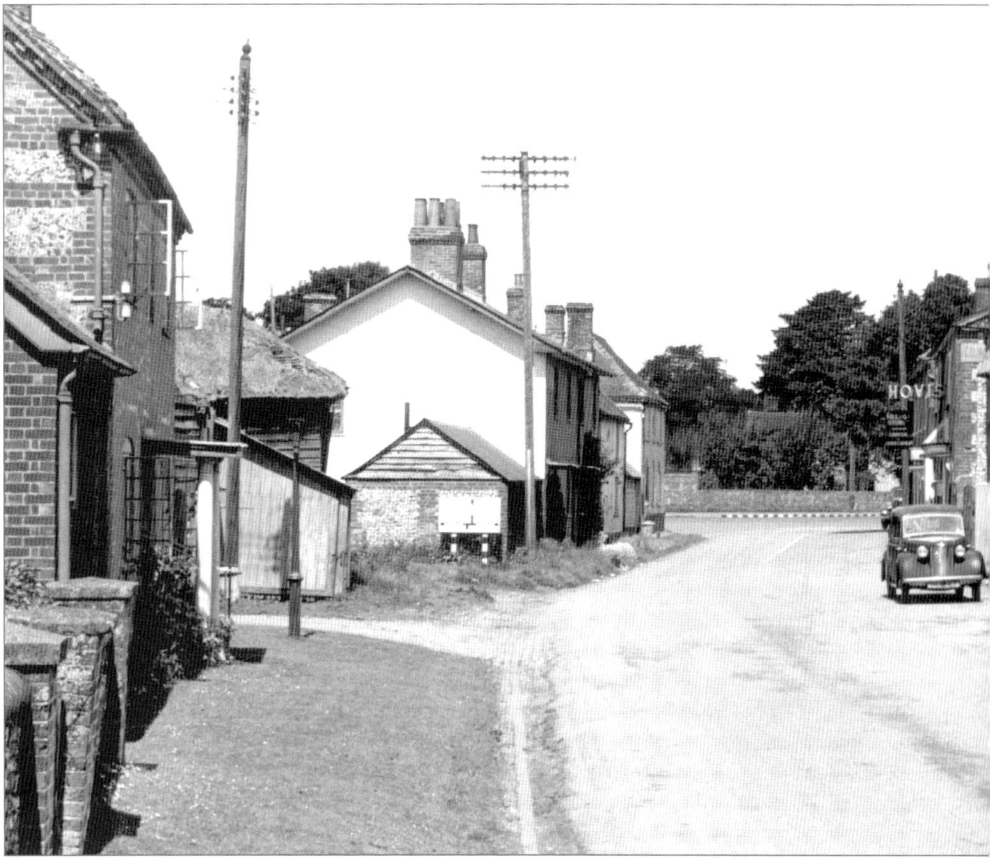

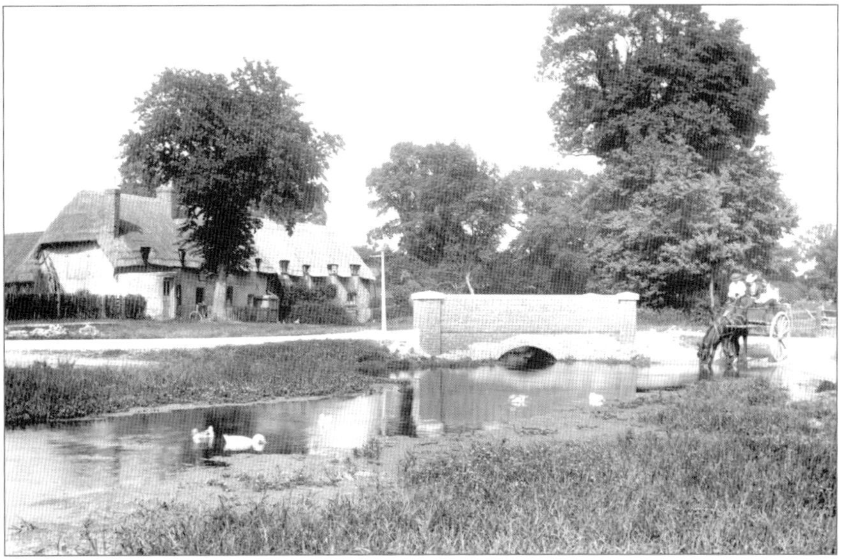

CHARLTON
The Village 1908 60101

This small village is now almost joined to Andover. Its church was moved, minus the tower, from neighbouring Foxcotte in Victorian times. Ducks forage and a horse slakes its thirst at the Andover Road bridge on the outskirts of Charlton, which at this date was quite distinct from the town. The nearest cottage and outbuildings have gone, but the freshly thatched pair remain. They were once a public house, the Buck and Dog.

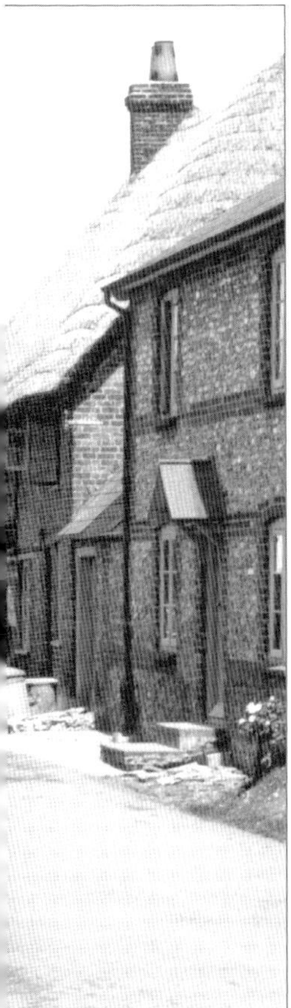

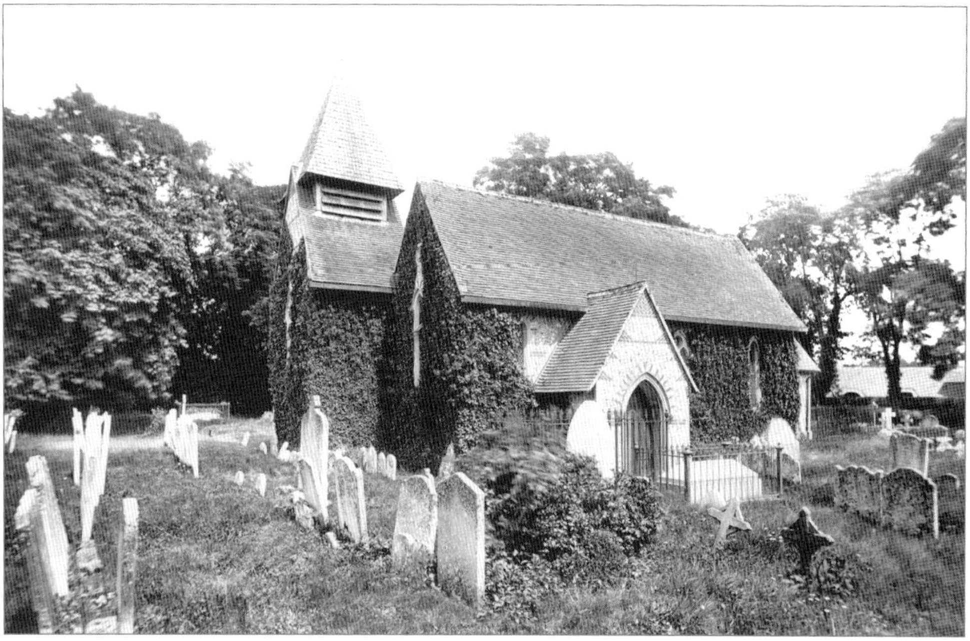

▲ **WEYHILL,** *The Church of St Michael and All Angels 1898* 42087

Weyhill's famous sheep fair took place at Michaelmas, when 100,000 beasts could be sold in one week. There were also horse, cheese, hop and pleasure fairs. The last sale of any note took place in 1957. In this photograph, nature seems determined to overwhelm the church and churchyard at Weyhill, and this just 30 years after a major restoration by the architect Hakewill. Only the porch provides a clear view of the flint and brick bands that characterise the building. The teetering grave markers add to the dishevelled air.

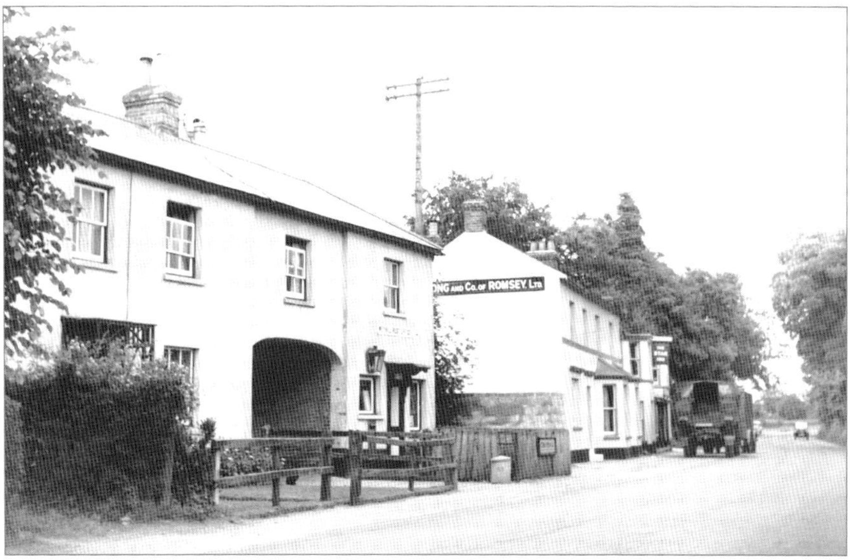

◄ **WEYHILL**
The Post Office
1950 W174009

This sleepy roadside settlement came to life every October when the Weyhill Sheep Fair, 'the greatest in the kingdom', assembled here. At the Star Inn next to the post office, ancient initiation ceremonies for apprentice shepherds took place, such as the 'horning of the colts'. The fair features as Weydon Priors in Hardy's 'The Mayor of Casterbridge'.

ANDOVER, *Church Hill 1955* A49014

Andover was an important market town in its early days, but grew little until it was selected in the 1960s to take some of London's overspill population. The impressive exterior of St Mary's Church, its sheer west tower of knapped flint and Caen stone enlivened by tall lancet bell openings, blank lancets, and high pinnacles, was part of a new building commissioned by Dr W S Goddard in the 1840s. Down below, the Pollen Almshouses of 1686, refurbished in 1872, use flint and brick to good effect.

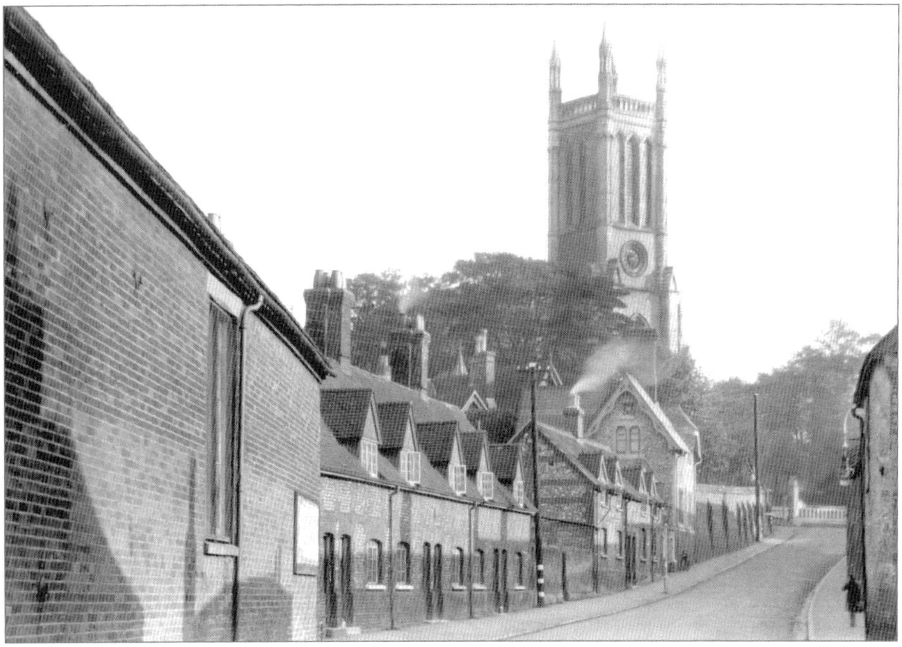

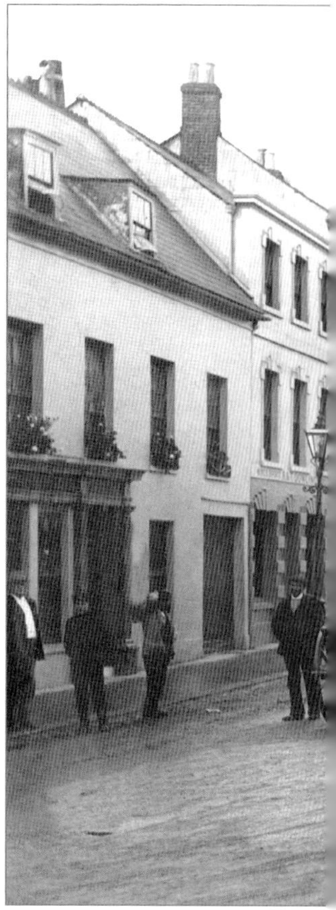

ANDOVER, *Winchester Street 1904* 52143

The days are numbered for Harvey's and the barber's next door (left) – they are still wearing a thatched roof, while the neighbours have all moved upmarket. Bell & Co's slogan, 'Cycle and Motor Depot', looks like a brand new message for a new age, but the street is still a safe place to loiter. On the right, a beef carcase hangs outside Noyce & Sons, the butchers, while their wares attract an attentive audience. The family traded in Andover from 1888 to 1968, with F R Noyce donning the mayoral robes in 1912, and also being second-in-command of the town's Fire Brigade.

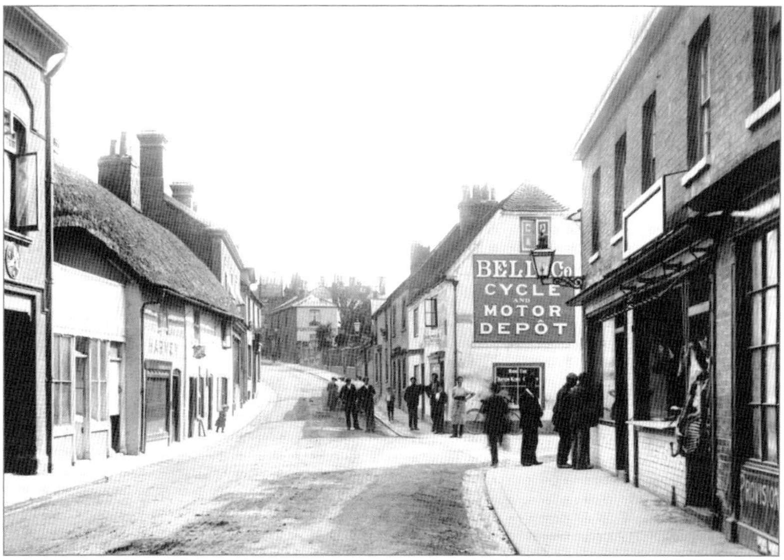

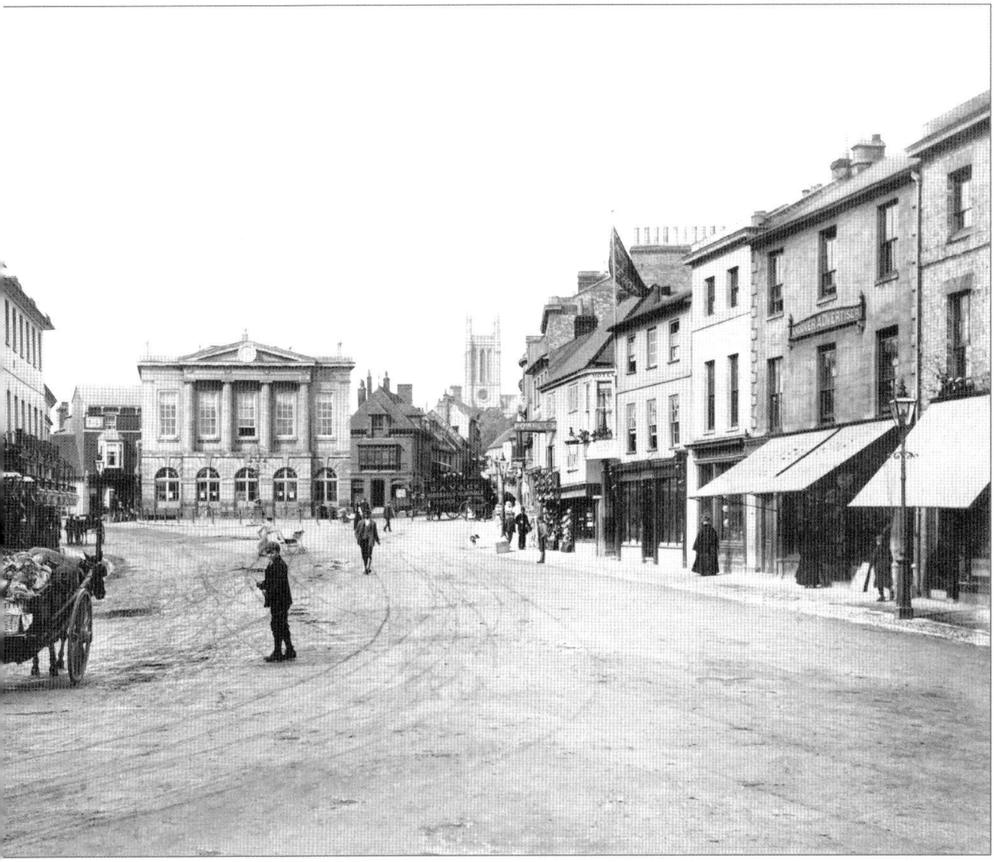

ANDOVER
High Street
1906 54615

The wide High Street allows an excellent view of the Palladian-style Guildhall of 1825, and is also able to accommodate the weekly market. More permanent businesses occupy the buildings on either side. Dowlings the wine merchants is visible behind the vegetable-laden donkey-cart (left). On the opposite flank, a stationer's (Holmes) and a shoe shop (Powney's) vie for the attention of the handful of shoppers.

ANDOVER
High Street
1955 A49060

Fifty years on, pride of place in the High Street goes to the motor car, and shoppers have to skip across the street for their own safety. Businesses now trumpet themselves and their wares more loudly. Woolworth's and Cooper's grocery are on the right; Holmes still hold court on the left, next to the Copper Kettle, Riggs the tobacconist's and the George Hotel.

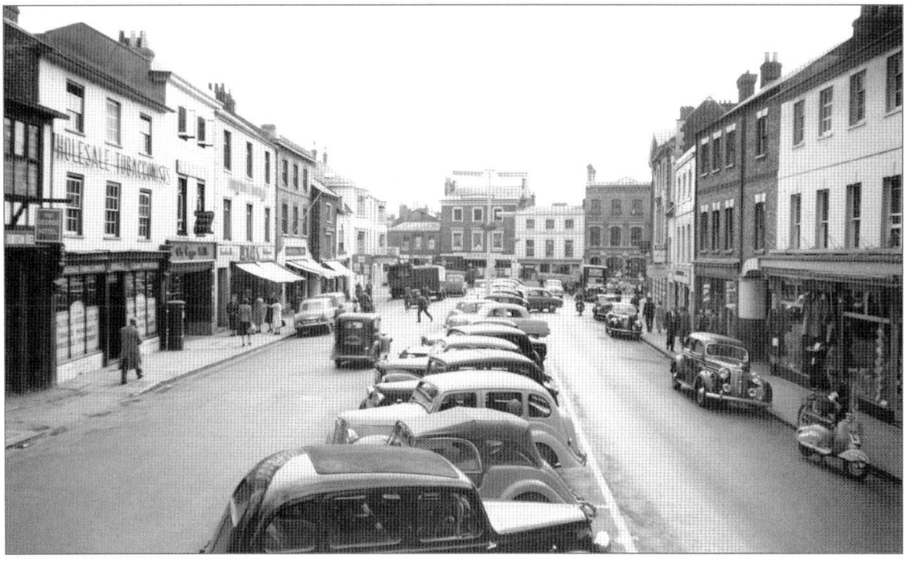

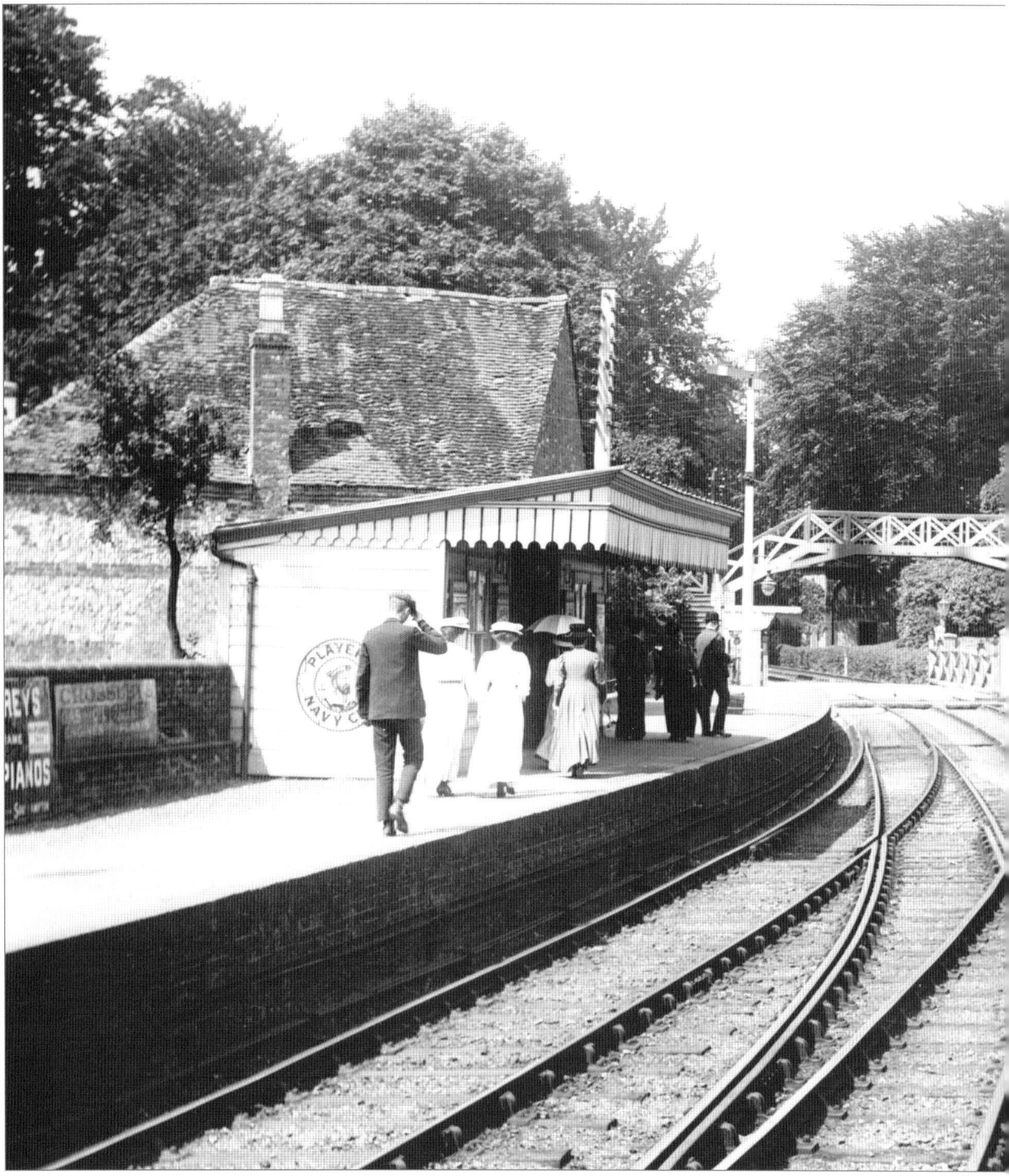
PIANOS

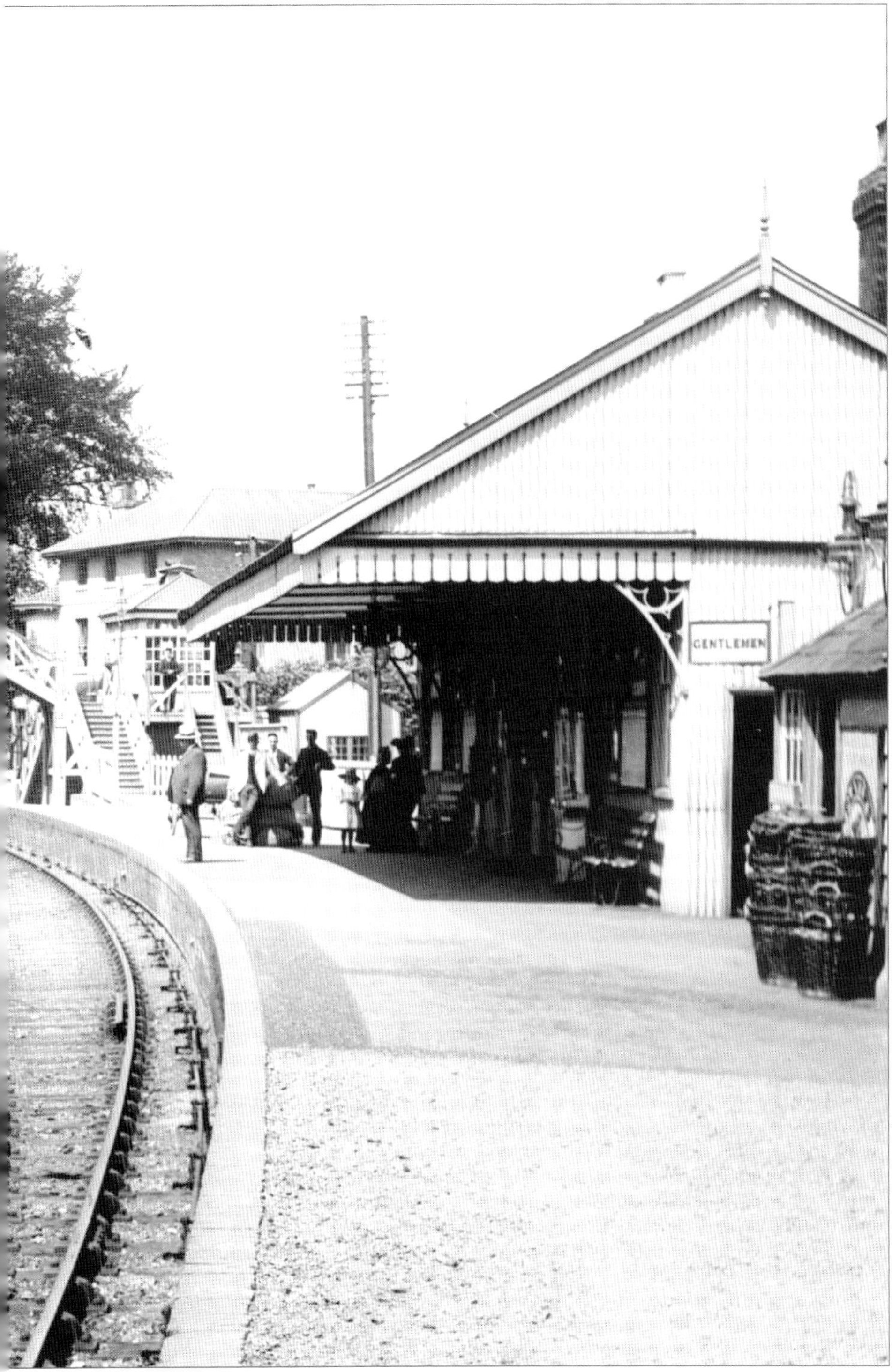

ANDOVER
Town Station
1908 60096

Elegant Edwardians stroll along the platform of the town station, the train from which they have alighted having disappeared towards the junction. On the opposite platform staff and passengers await the return working, and the signalman surveys the scene from his balcony. The Town Station on the 'Sprat and Winkle' line, as it was known, opened in 1865 and closed 99 years later. This was the line that served Clatford, Fullerton, and Stockbridge, and then further stations to Romsey. It proved extremely popular with Andoverians who wished to travel down the Test Valley for summer walks and picnics.

ANDOVER, *The Town Mill 1908* 60095

The Anton flows peacefully towards the town bridge and the wide expanse of the old ford, regularly used for watering cattle and horses. Beyond the man standing at the water's edge, and the tailrace joining the river on the left, stands the Town Mill, recorded in Domesday but dated, in its pictured form, by plaques of 1752 and 1764.

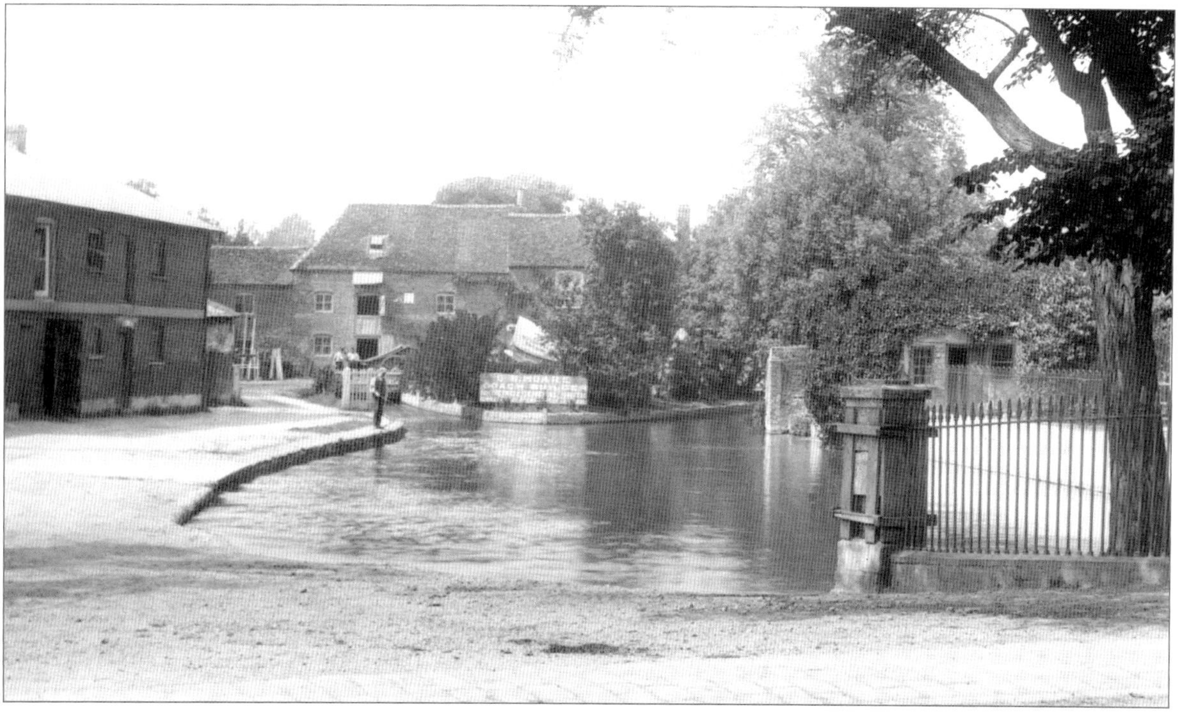

THRUXTON, *The Church of St Peter and St Paul 1898* 42089

Thruxton is a large village with many thatched cottages, and is best known these days for its motor racing circuit. Thruxton church, a Norman foundation, has acquired elements of Decorated and Perpendicular styles over time, and also a squat classical stone tower, built in 1801 because its predecessor collapsed. Victorian restoration took place in 1869. This view shows to good effect the enormous flints used in the body of the church, and the beautifully tended churchyard, full of trees and shrubs.

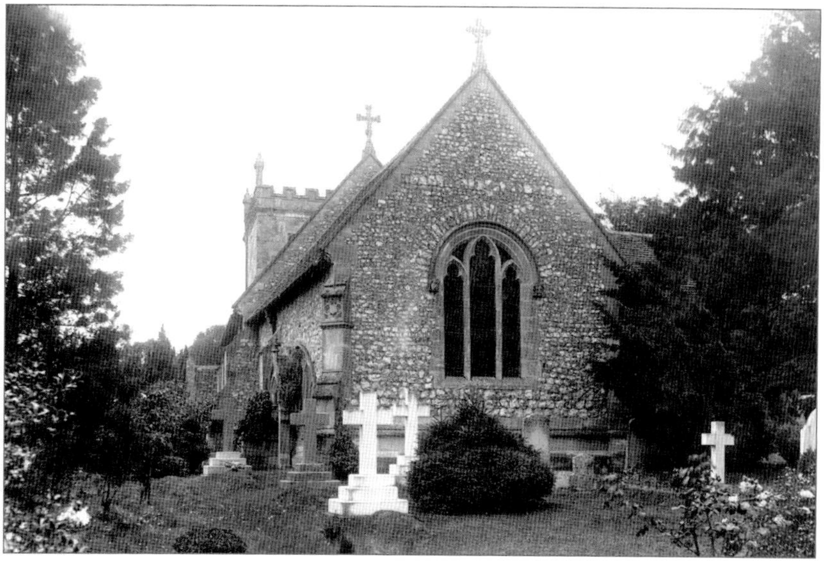

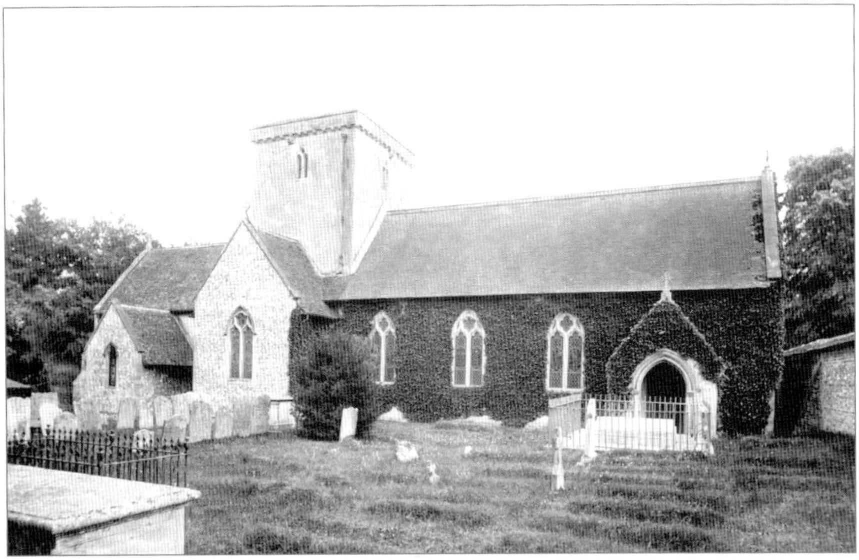

AMPORT, *St Mary's Church 1898* 42091

The flint and stone church is cruciform in plan with a central tower. The original construction of 1320-30 was plain, but ballflower ornament around the parapet and flamboyant window tracery bestow Decorated-style status. Much of the early fabric was retained during Slater and Carpenter's sympathetic restoration of 1886-87. In the churchyard, memorial stones and tombs contrast dramatically with the serried ranks of unmarked graves.

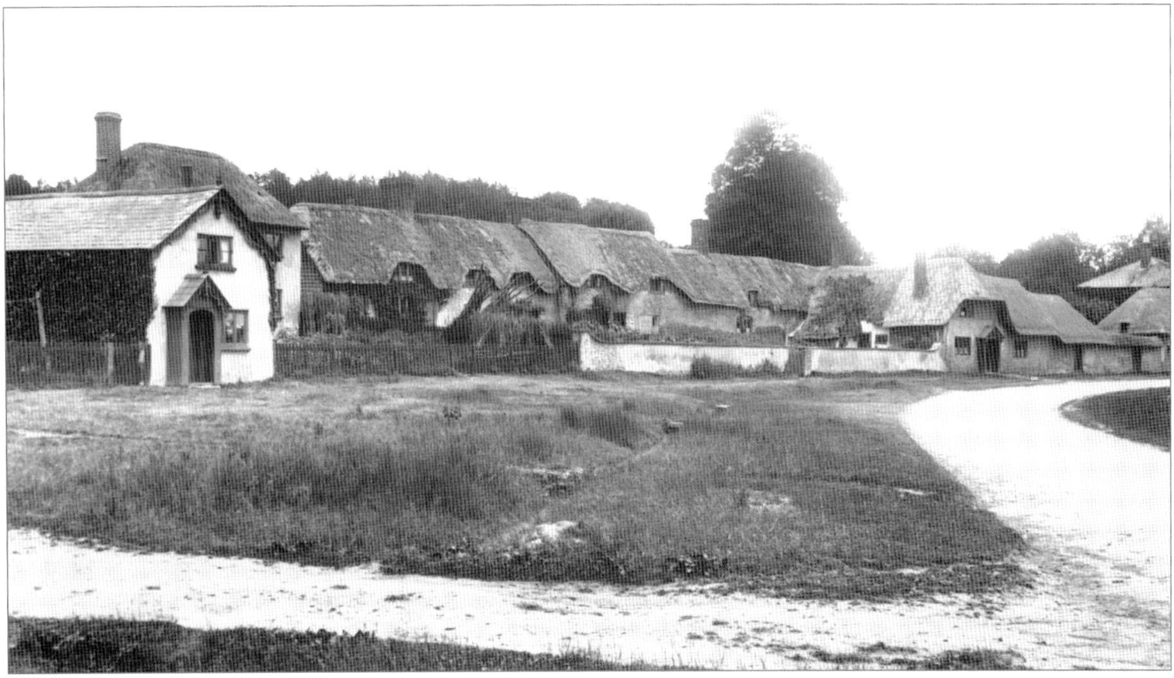

AMPORT, *The Village 1898* 42092

Amport lies in the valley of the Pillhill Brook. It benefited from many charitable acts in the past, particularly those by Sophia Routh. As we can see from this photograph, Amport boasts a large informal green, the scene of maypole dancing on Old May Day, 12 May, for nearly 200 years. An eclectic group of houses and cottages stand on one side. In this view the tiled roof of the Old Farm contrasts with its thatched neighbours, which include Willow Cottage, dated 1711. Ornamental bargeboards abound.

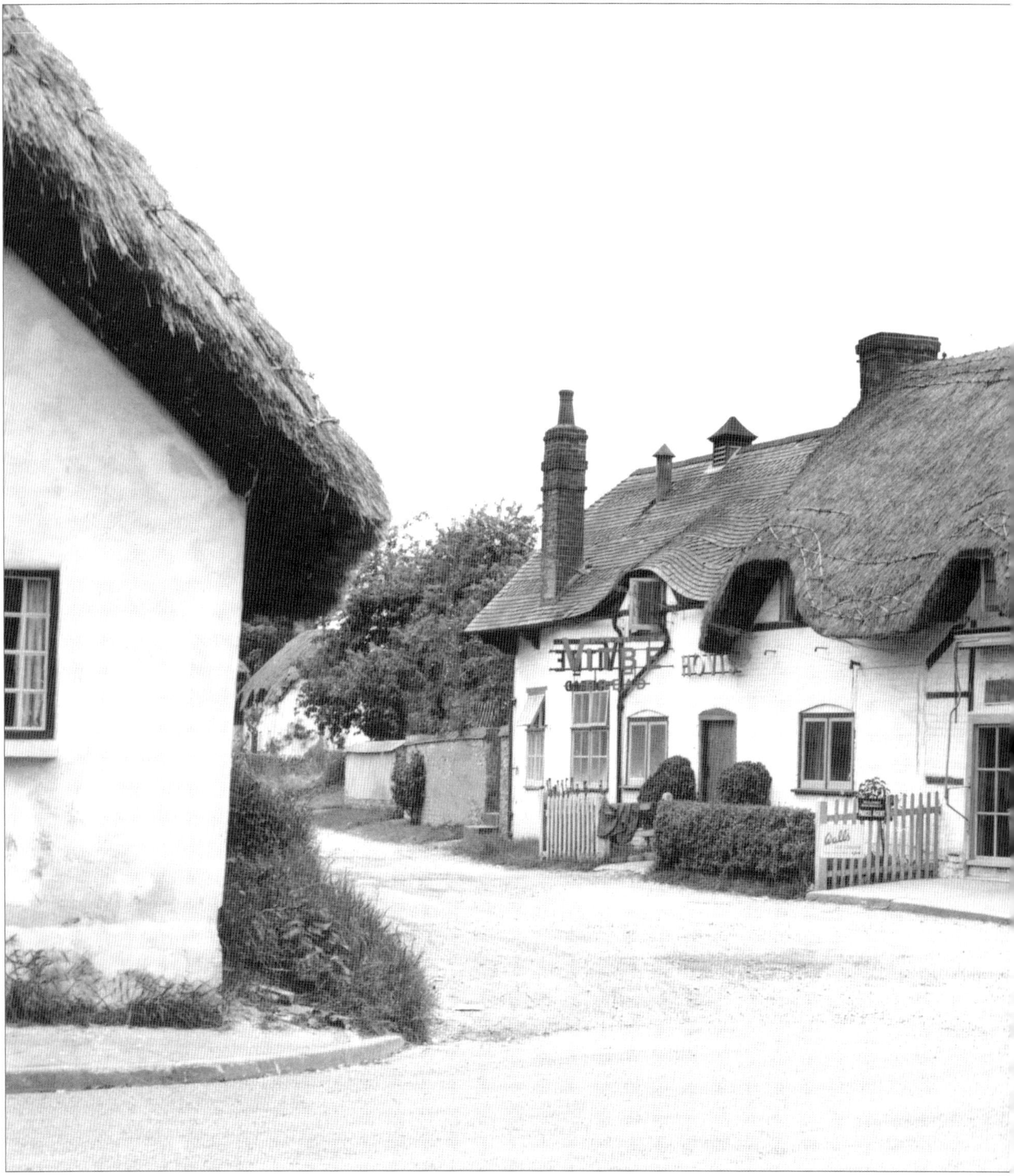

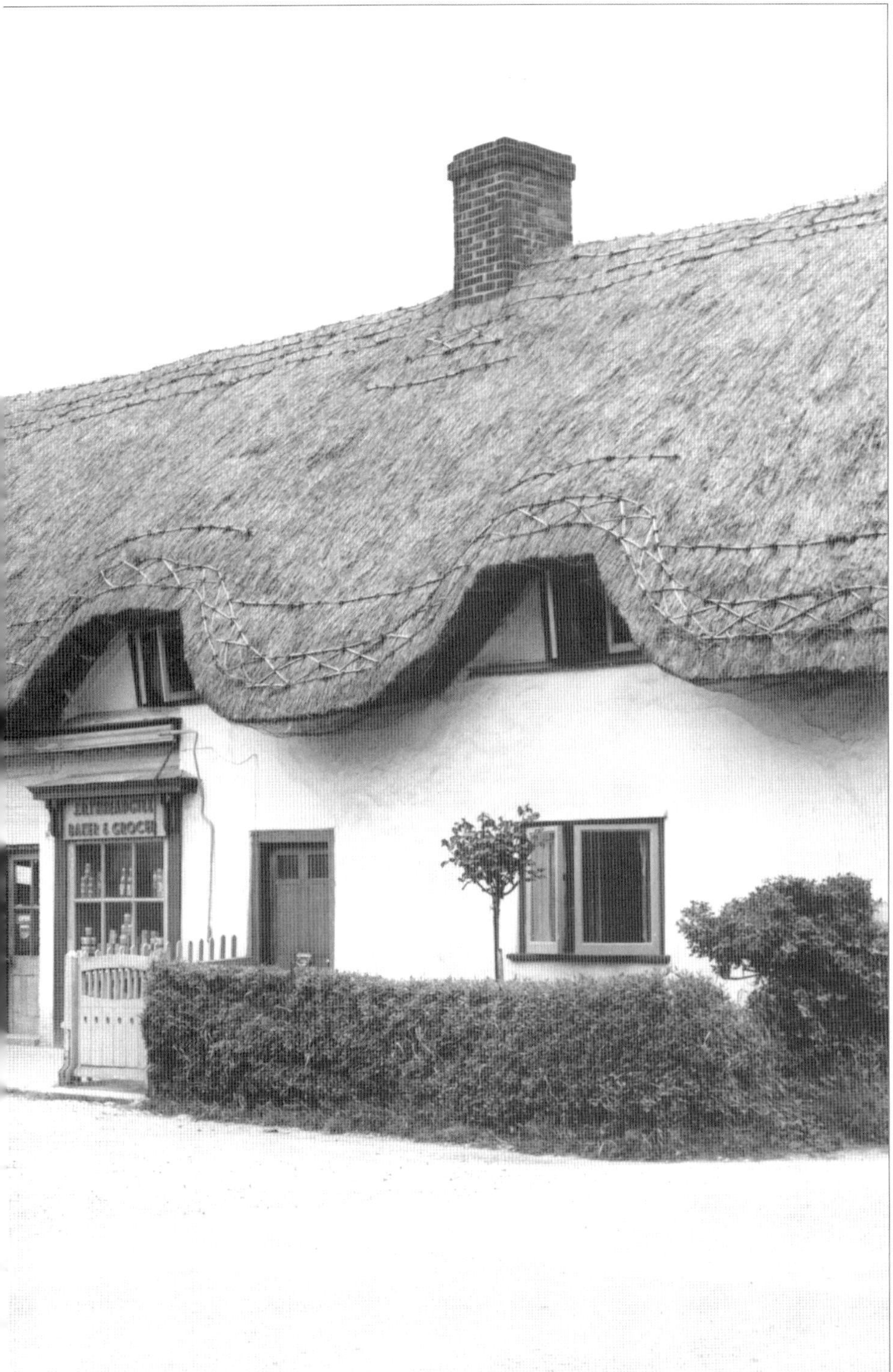

ABBOTTS ANN
The Village 1960 A4008

Abbotts Ann is a large village with many thatched cottages, a number of which make effective use of banded flint and brick panels. J D Threadgill, 'Baker & Grocer', advertising Hovis bread and Walls ice cream, stood at the corner of Dunkirt ('dung cart') Lane, so-called because it was the route by which 'night soil' was taken to the fields. Jesse Threadgill arrived at Abbotts Ann in 1902 to be an apprentice coachbuilder. Ten years later he took over the bakery during an illustrious career, which eventually saw him Chairman of Andover Rural District Council. His delightfully smart premises are timber-framed and rendered with a thatched roof. The roof of the bakery (left), with its tall chimney and vents, is tiled.

▼ **ABBOTTS ANN,** *St Mary's Church 1899* 43696

The church was built in 1716 thanks to the proceeds from the sale of a huge diamond to the Regent of France by Thomas 'Diamond' Pitt, one-time Governor of Madras. Its plain style makes excellent use of light brick (much hidden by ivy in this photograph) with stone cornices and angle pilasters. The west tower sports Victorian pinnacles, each with its own wind vane, and the east windows have Victorian tracery. The west windows retain their earlier form. Inside are many original fittings, as well as the renowned 'Virgins' Crowns', carried at the funerals of those who were born, baptised and confirmed in the parish, and died unmarried.

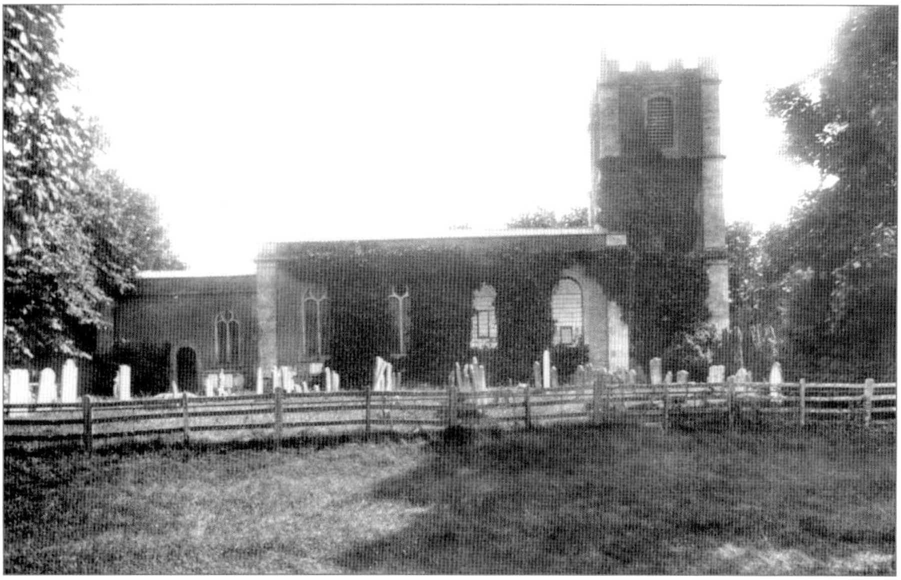

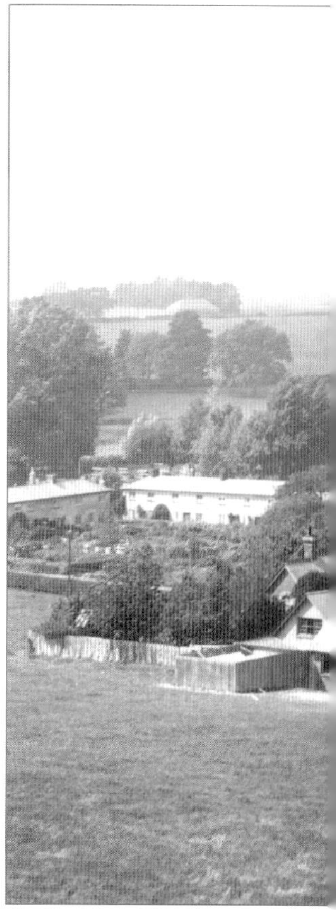

► **ABBOTTS ANN**
The Village 1960 A4013

Thatched roofs and flint walls with red brick bands and dressings abound in this view looking north along the main street. The exception is the Eagle public house, which can be glimpsed between the two plain telegraph poles, pointing its brick-built gable ends and tiled roofs towards the bus shelter, pub sign and road.

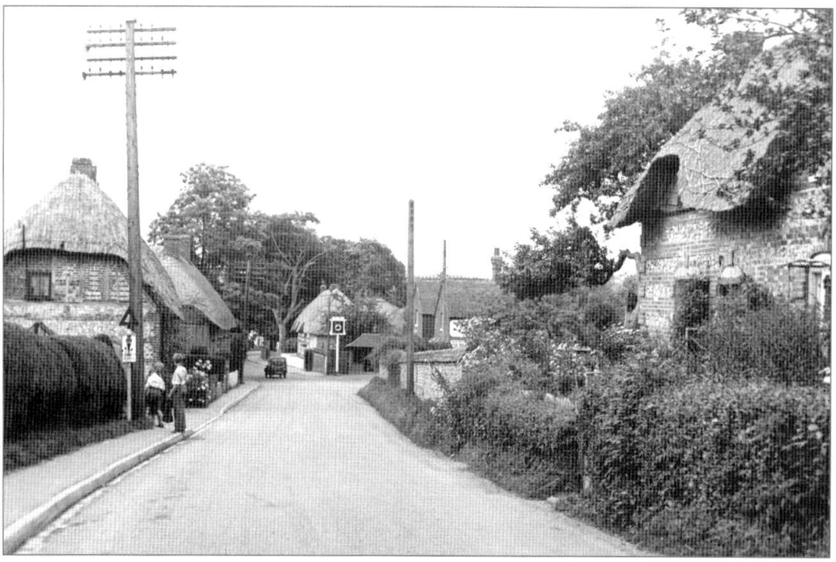

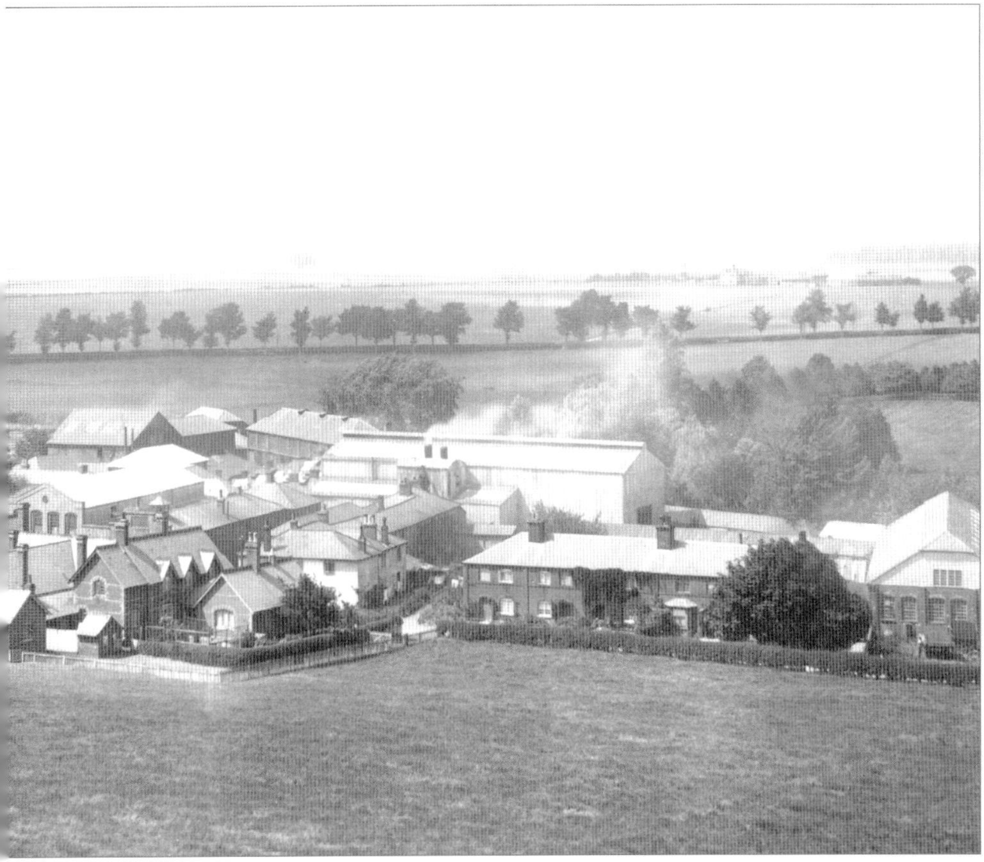

◄ **ANNA VALLEY**
The Foundry
1899 43695

Robert Tasker set up in business as a blacksmith in Abbotts Ann in 1809 and four years later founded what was to become the Waterloo Ironworks in nearby Anna Valley. By the end of the century it had spread to cover 11 acres and employed 300 men, many of whom were housed in the 37 cottages built and owned by the firm.

► **ANNA VALLEY**
Tasker's Works
c1955 A53008

It is all quiet outside Tasker's imposing showroom frontage of 1891, except for a lone cyclist on the valley road and two women, one with babe in arms, making their way towards the post office. This building was formerly the Plough public house, but Tasker's influence – he favoured temperance and abstinence - saw it closed. The post office shut up shop in 1956.

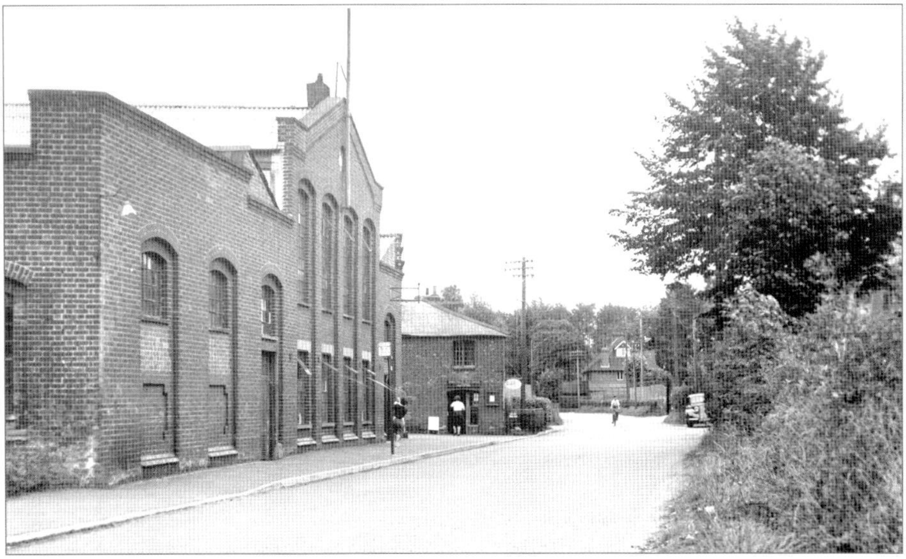

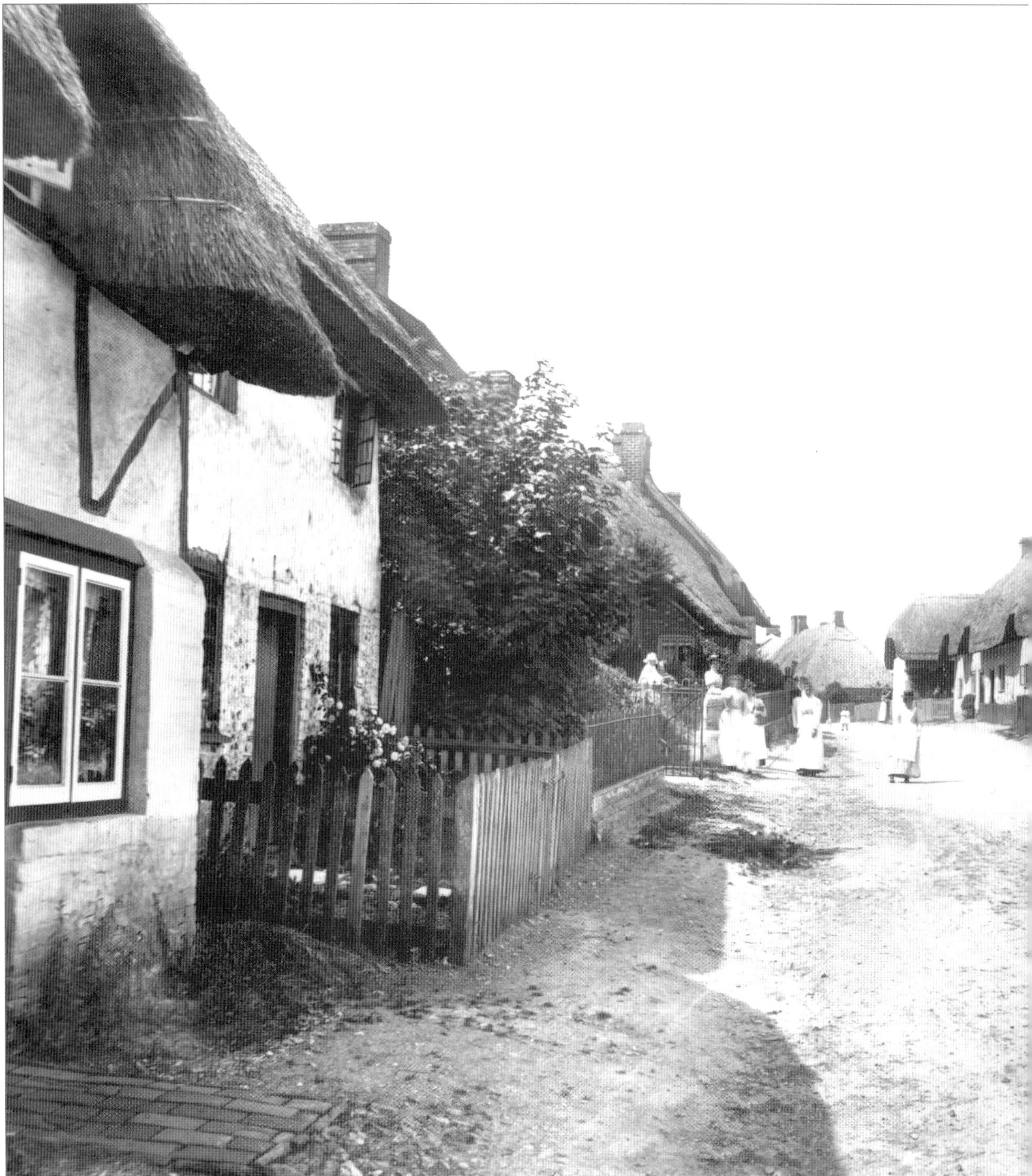

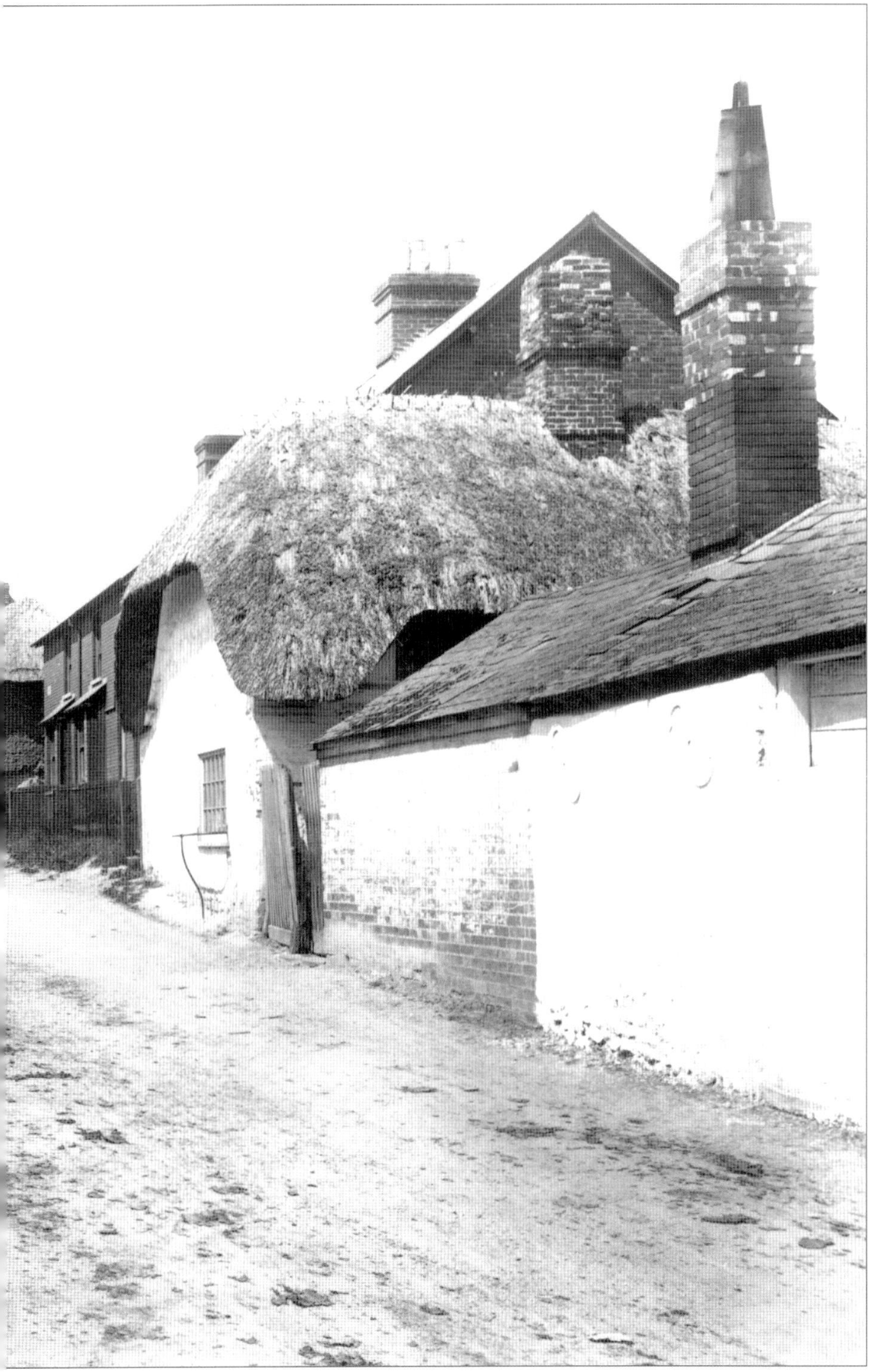

UPPER CLATFORD
The Village 1899 43693

The name Clatford means 'ford where the burdock grows'. Goodworth Clatford was formerly named Lower Clatford. In this photograph, a group of women, some with white starched aprons, have emerged to take an interest in the photographer's work, while keeping a respectable distance. Across the street an angular terrace of brick houses, built by Tasker's in 1888, contrasts with the dumpy collection of thatched cottages of earlier date. The first building on the left is the Crook and Shears.

ANNA VALLEY, *Red Rice School c1965* A53015

Red Rice is attributed to General Webb, who fought at Malplaquet, and trees in the park were said to represent the lines of troops at that battle, but the date of construction is supposedly 1740, and Webb died in 1724! The house was rebuilt along classical lines in 1844; the façade is thirteen bays wide, although the porte cochère (carriage entrance) of four Tuscan columns is not central. Among its famous visitors was the Prince of Wales (later George IV), on the trail of Mrs Fitzherbert, and General Eisenhower in 1944. In 1961 it became an independent school for boys, and some of them can be seen playing sports in the field (centre left).

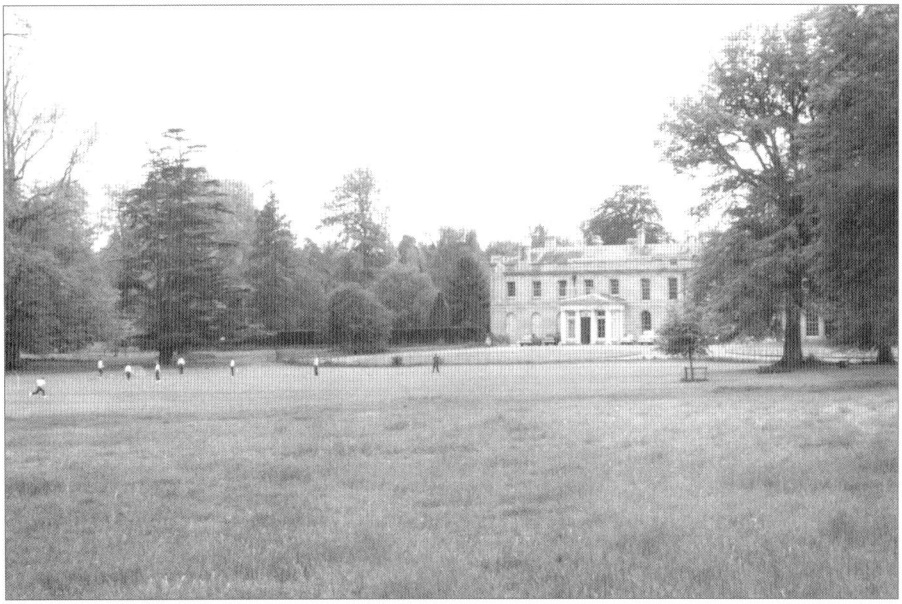

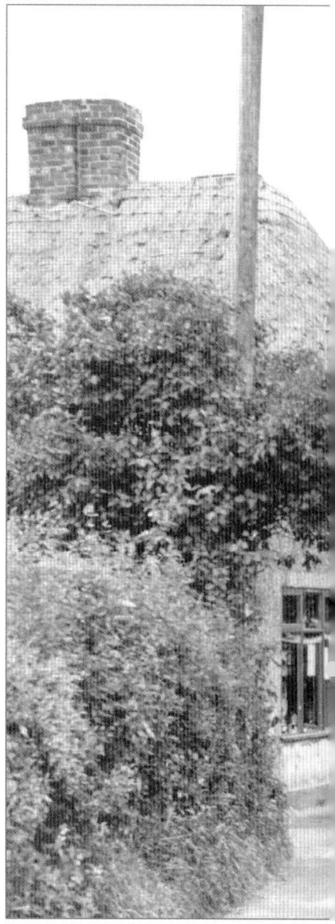

UPPER CLATFORD
All Saints' Church 1899 43694

The oldest elements of this church are of 12th-century Norman date, but are rather lost beneath 17th-century rearrangements and an enlarged chancel of 1890. Repairs to the tower, which is partly hidden by the trees, are dated by two fragments of inscribed stone: 'Repaired in the Year of the Lord 1578'.

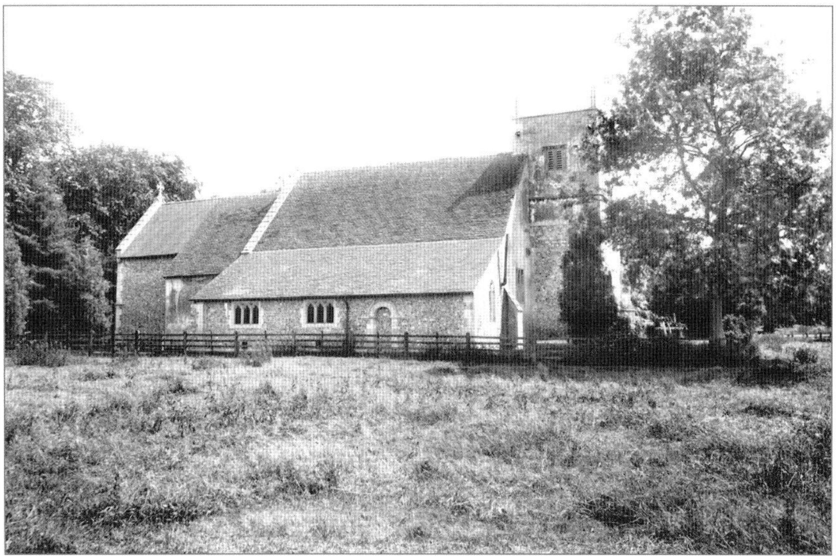

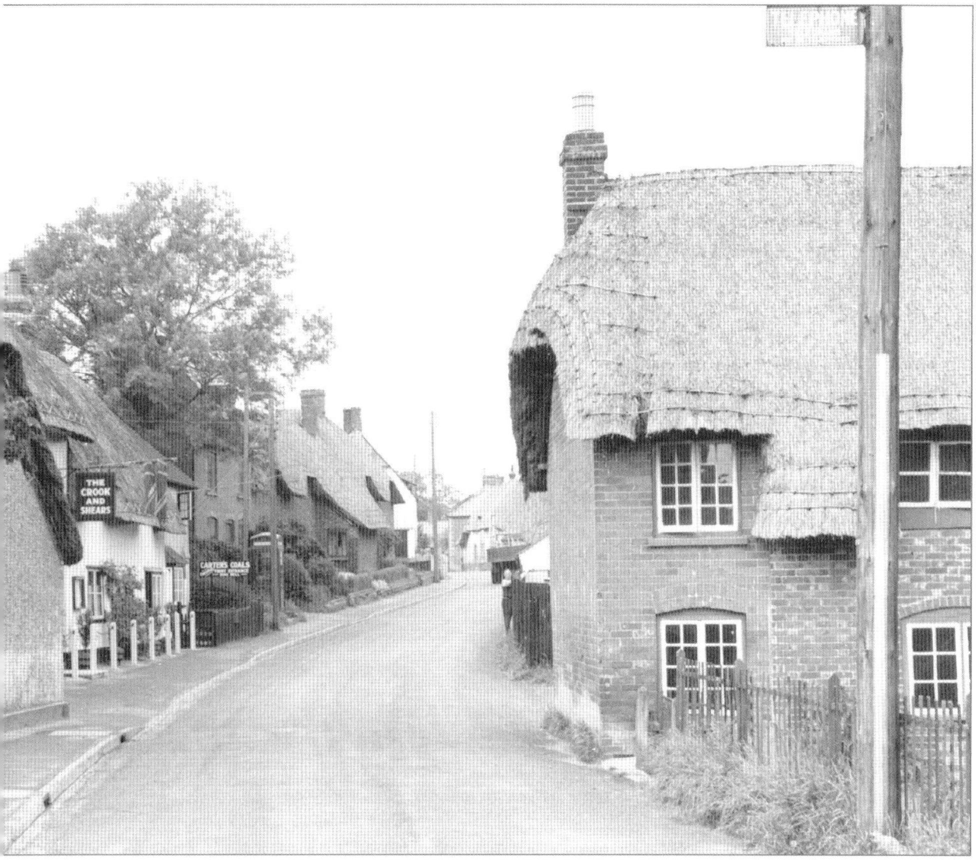

UPPER CLATFORD
The Village
c1955 U53006

Fifty years after 43693 (pages 28-29) was taken, this area was clearly a centre of commerce for the village. The post office is on the left, having moved from just across the road. Next comes the Crook and Shears, Upper Clatford's most enduring pub, and finally Carter's coals, paraffin and other fuels are advertised on a board in front of the telephone kiosk.

UPPER CLATFORD
Fishing Cottage
1955 U53001

When George Fowle joined William Tasker at the Waterloo Ironworks in 1836 the number of structural products increased dramatically. The most notable examples were cast-iron bridges, and Clatford has two. Spanning the River Anton next to the elegantly refurbished Fishing Cottage is a little gem, with ornate roundels in the spandrels. It was cast in 1843.

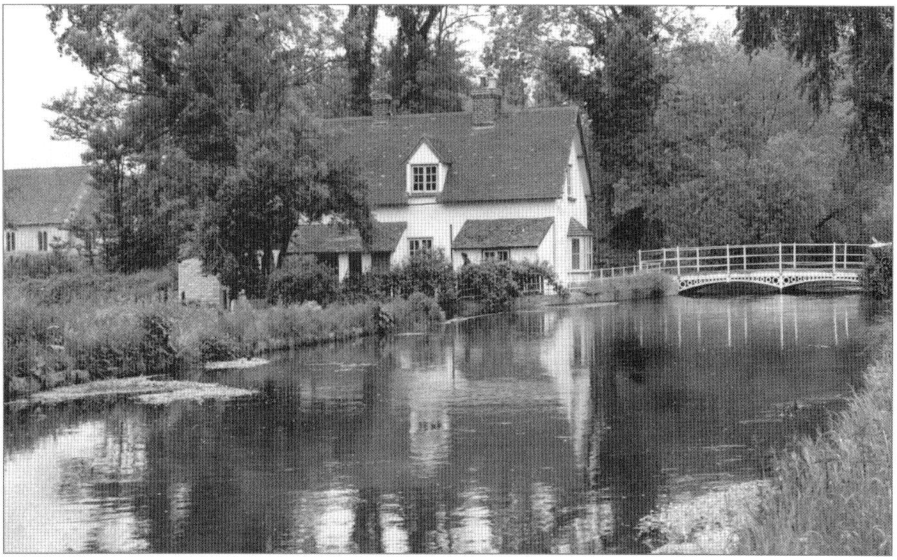

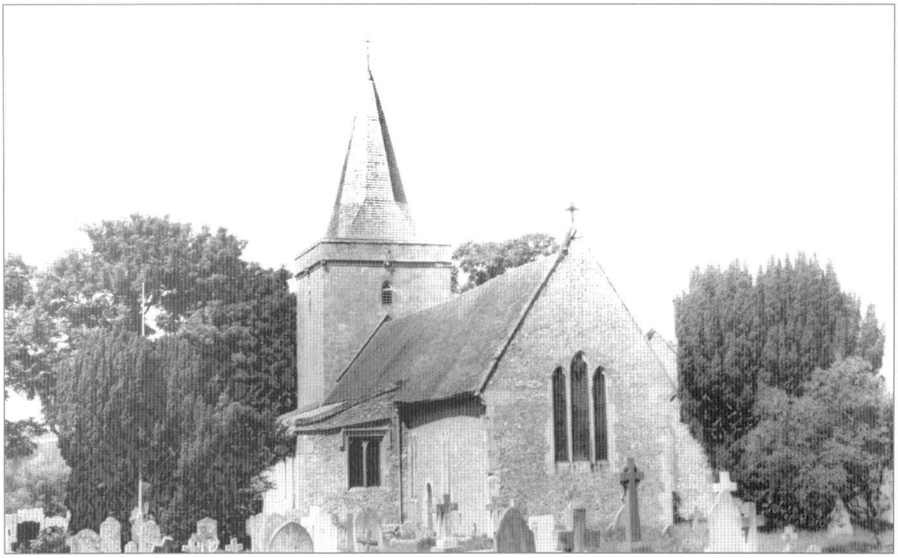

GOODWORTH CLATFORD
St Peter's Church 1965 G87006

This small church, sitting among a forest of grave markers, may have Saxon origins; it was a dependency of Wherwell Abbey until the Dissolution of the Monasteries. It has early Norman pillars in the nave and there are Norman fragments in the 13th-century stone tower, but this has been topped with a Victorian shingled spire.

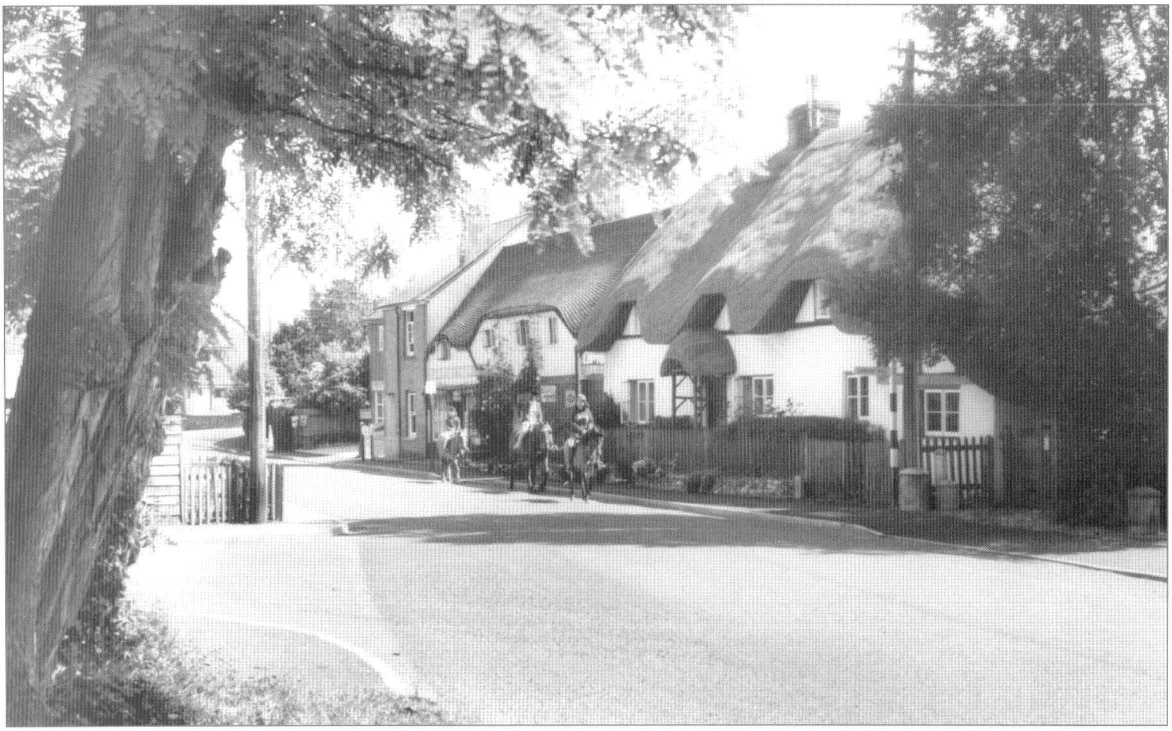

GOODWORTH CLATFORD, *The Village 1965* G87001

The riders and ponies have just passed the post office and stores (the postmistress at this date was Mrs E Taylor), and can either cross the road to head up Barrow Hill or, as seems more likely, carry on gently past Molesley Cottage and through the village. Galvanised bins lurk in the shadows; perhaps the dustcart is due later.

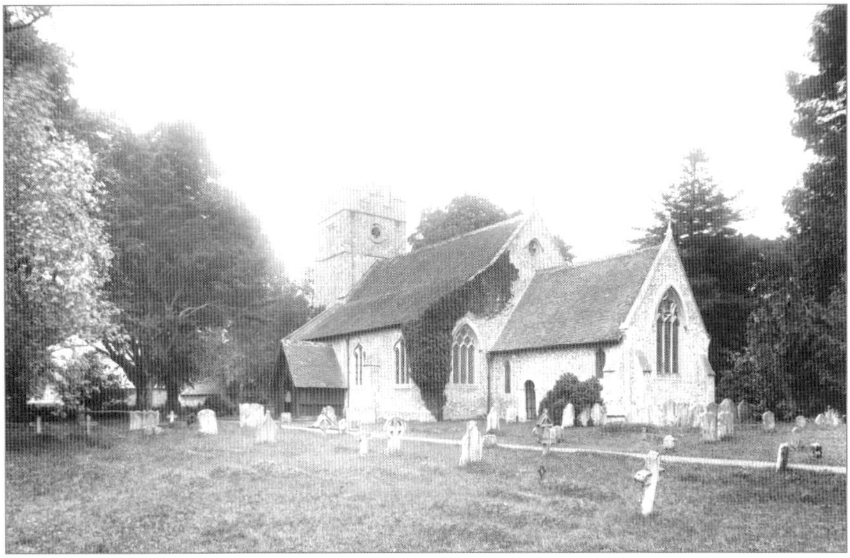

LONGPARISH
St Nicholas's Church 1899 43700

Longparish is indeed a long parish, with hamlets named Easton, Middleton and Forton. In former times the chief of these was Middleton. The most striking feature of this church is the Perpendicular west tower of chequered flint and stone built in the 15th century, with its small crenellated look-out point. The tower was inserted into the existing nave, which is of the 11th and 12th century. Victorian restoration took place in 1857.

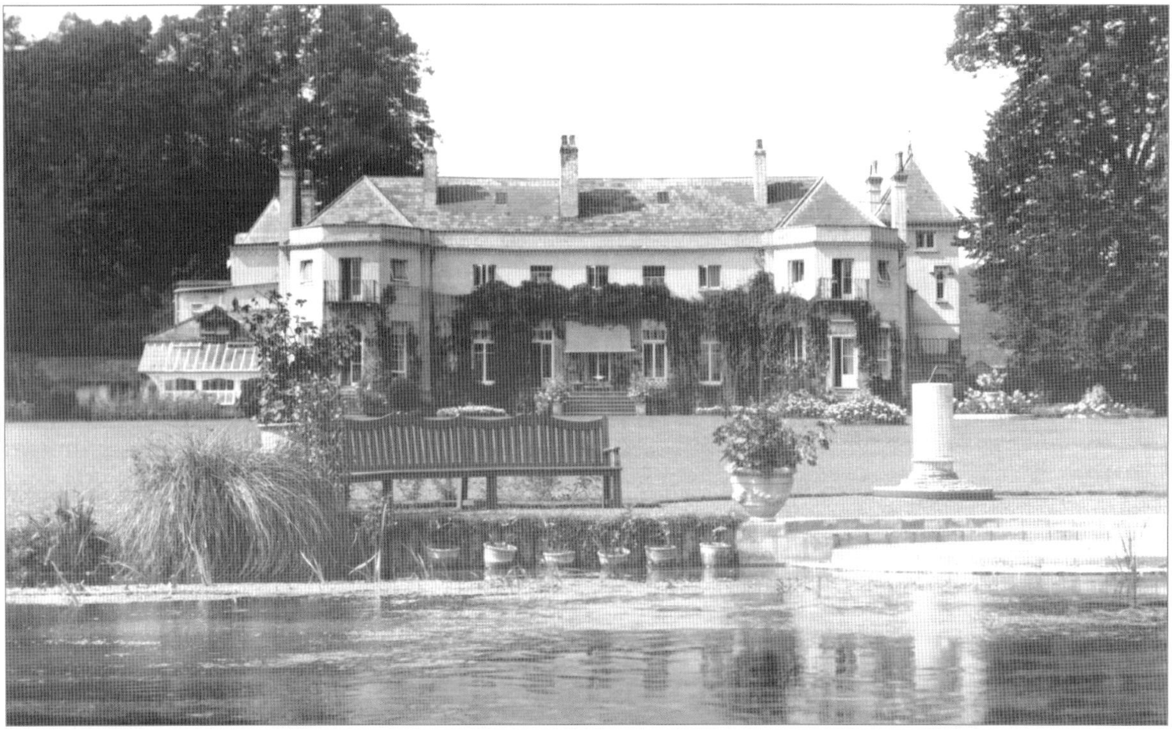

LONGPARISH, *Longparish House 1960* L220001

This fine house, with stuccoed walls and turrets at either end in the style of a French chateau, has an exquisite riverside setting. It was home in the 19th century to Colonel Peter Hawker, famous for his sporting diaries of 1809 to 1853, which detail the birds, beasts and fish that he bagged with rod and gun. The garden seat and sundial (on the column to the right) bring to mind more leisurely, reflective pursuits.

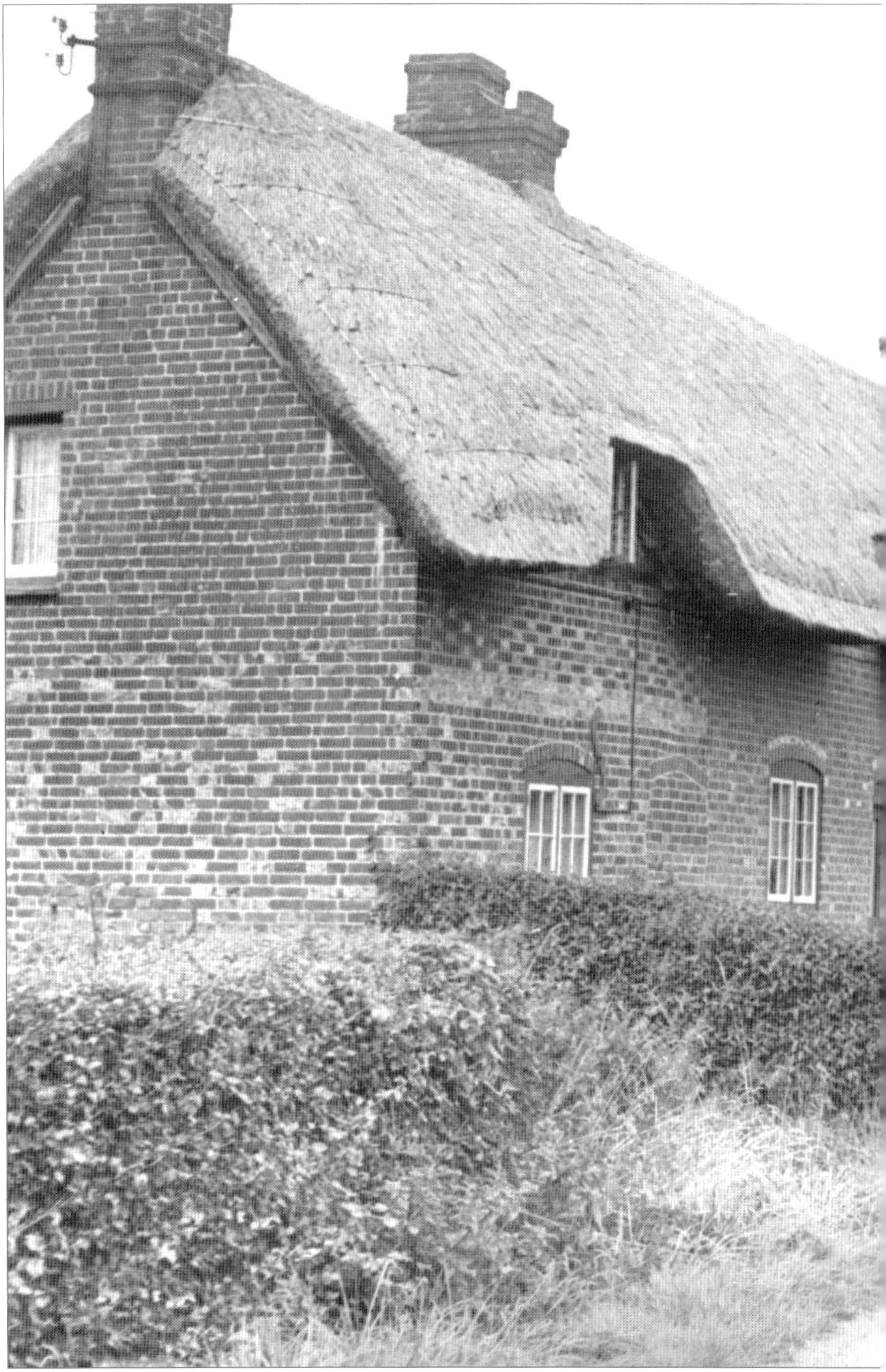

LONGPARISH
The Main Road
1960 L220007

Longparish is a long village, meandering for two miles alongside the Test, but it was originally called Middleton, a name that survives as a hamlet and an estate. Typical Longparish cottages are Aston Cottage, in the foreground, and its neighbours. Today the little girls will be well over 40, and Aston Cottage is painted white.

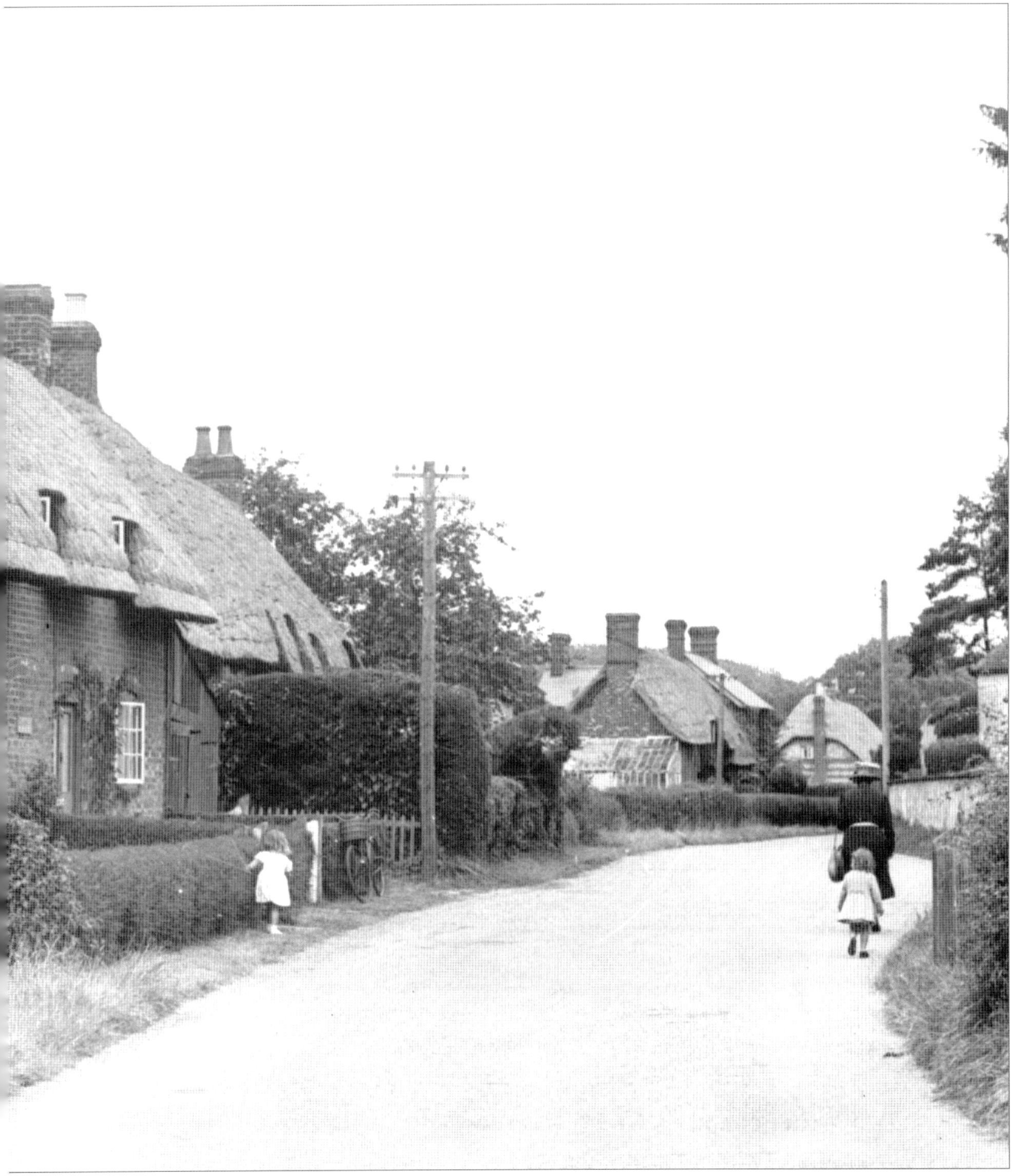

▼ **FORTON,** *The Village 1955* F226021

By contrast with Longparish, Forton is a small semicircular hamlet of cottages close to the river. Most of the houses began life as two dwellings, but many have been amalgamated into one. This is the case with Kingfisher Cottage on the right, with its exposed timber frame and limewashed brick infilling. In the distance is a fine example of a thatched pentice – the roof swoops down almost to ground level.

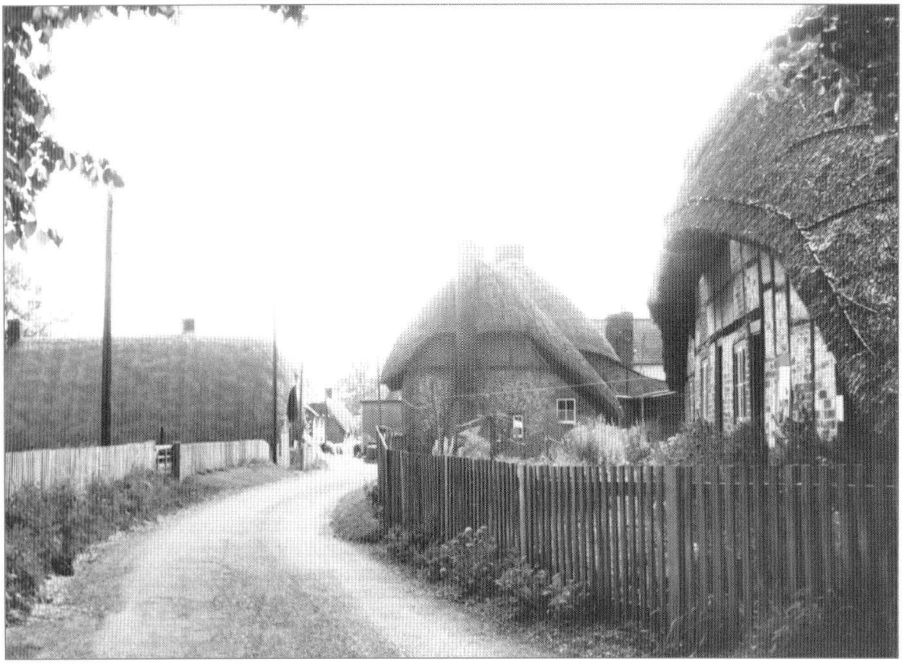

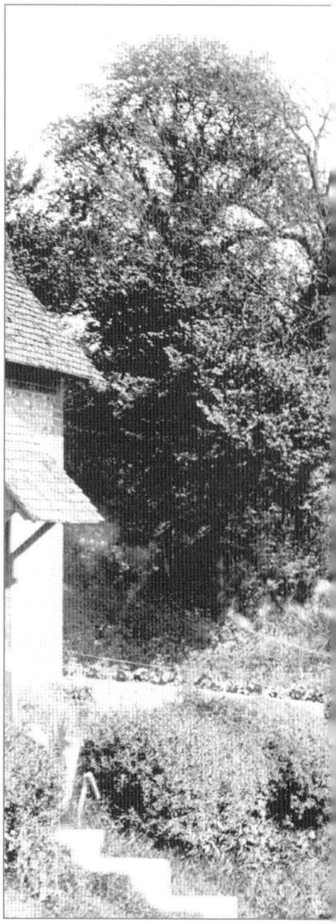

▶ **WHERWELL**
The Church of St Peter and Holy Cross 1901 46355

The picturesque thatched village of Wherwell stands near the site of a 10th-century nunnery. Recent survey work has found some of the conventual buildings surviving as outbuildings to The Priory, a house built in the 19th century. The 1856-58 restoration of St Peter's Church by Woodyer bestowed a rather spirited Scandinavian-style bell turret with a spire and a multitude of windows on this flint and Bath stone structure, with its red tiled roof. Tomb fragments and other reminders of Wherwell Abbey are to be found in the church, and were once built into the churchyard wall.

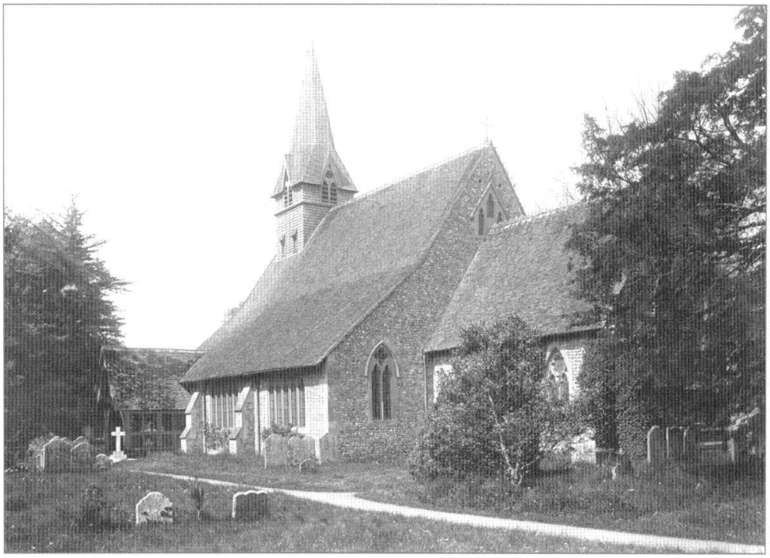

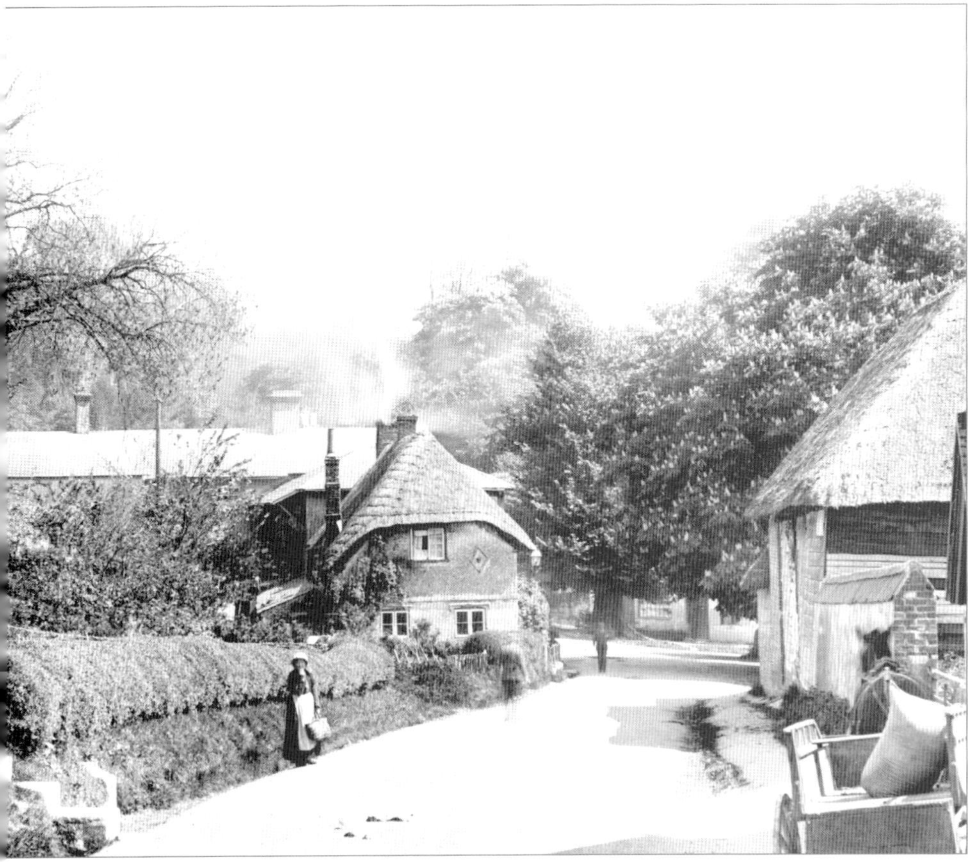

WHERWELL
The Village
1901 46353

Wherwell is considered to be one of Hampshire's prettiest villages. Its thatched cottages and barns cling close to the road between steep tree-covered slopes to the north and the river and The Priory to the south. In this view a woman pauses, or poses for the camera, while a man with no time to waste is off down the High Street towards Chestnut Cottage, in a sort of ghostly progression. On the right a horse tethered to a cart delivering seed corn to Manor Farm is also showing its impatience or, on such a sunny day, simply shaking off the flies.

WHERWELL
The Village
c1955 W78007

Fifty years after 46353 (above) was taken, the road is well surfaced and marked; but this scene, at the junction with Church Street, is still tranquil. Here the 'bosky combe' that the village inhabits can be appreciated, but the celebrated tree to the right is no more; it became too big for its roots.

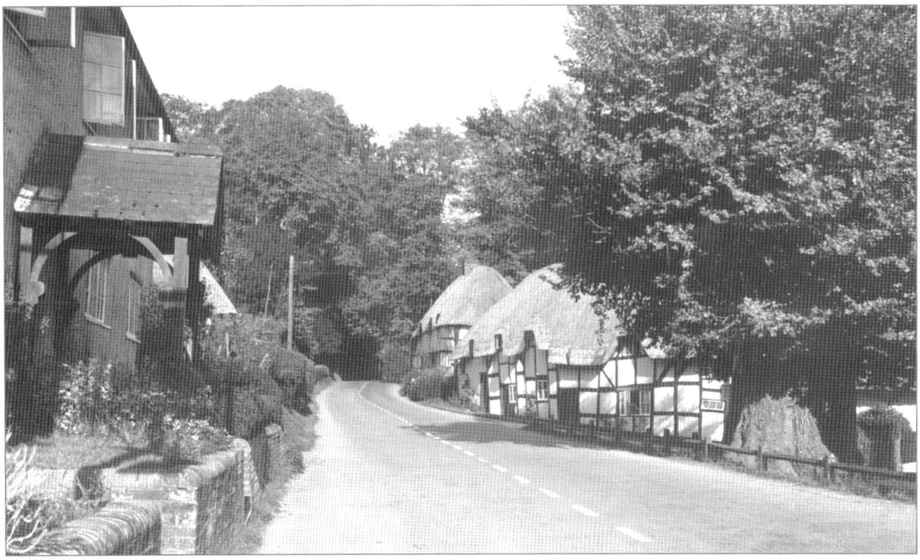

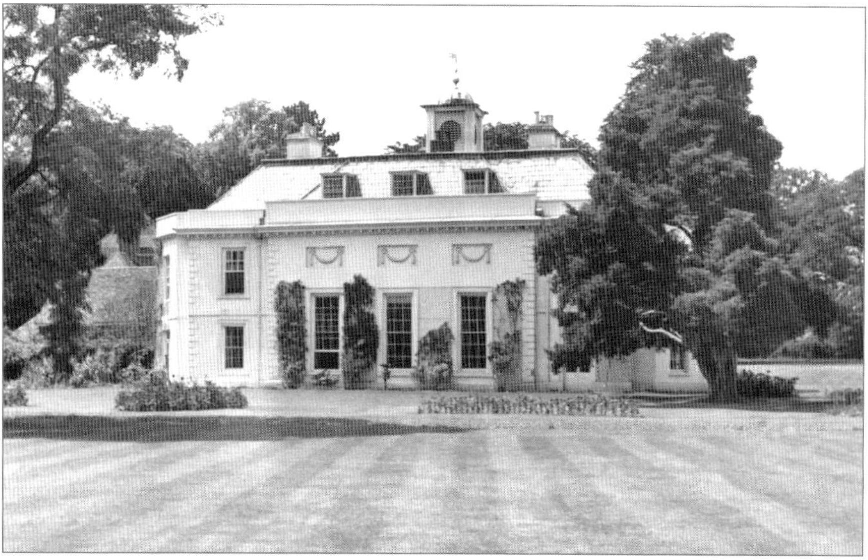

WHERWELL
The Priory
c1955 W78037

This white, stuccoed early 19th-century house is built on the site of Wherwell Abbey, and more particularly above a watercourse constructed by the Abbess Euphemia in the 13th century to improve sanitation and 'carry off all refuse that might corrupt the air'. The east front, seen here, is notable for the three middle windows, which span both ground and first floors to illuminate the dining room. On the roof is a domed cupola.

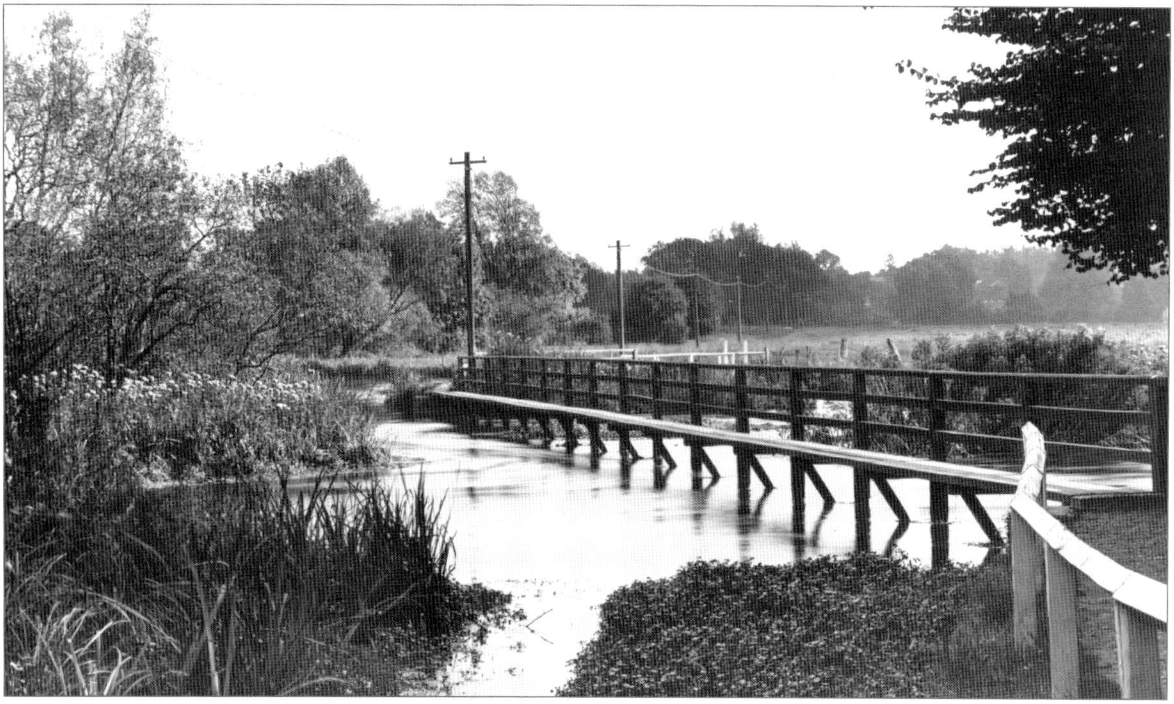

WHERWELL, *The Bridge over the River Test c1955* W78003

Sixty years ago a traveller relates how he was directed 'out onto the 'carmon' across a long bridge by the very beautiful tryst of the Test with a Wherwell stream, to a great expanse of marsh and water meadow'. Chilbolton Common, never ploughed or chemically treated, and a haven for wildlife, forms the backdrop to this view. Purlygig (or whirlpool) Bridge leads the way there.

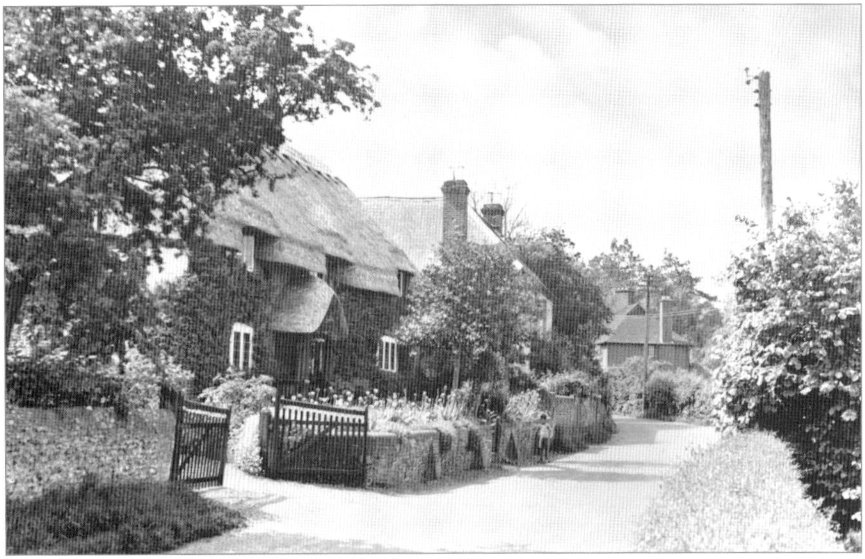

CHILBOLTON
St Michael's Cottage c1965 C227016

Chilbolton is a large village with many thatched cottages and access to Common and Down. Here, the small Chilbolton child is well camouflaged against the garden wall as he poses for the photographer. He is standing beside St Michael's Cottage, built of red brick with blue headers, with timber framing and plaster infill on the gable end, just visible through the trees. The ornate thatch, incorporating the porch, looks new.

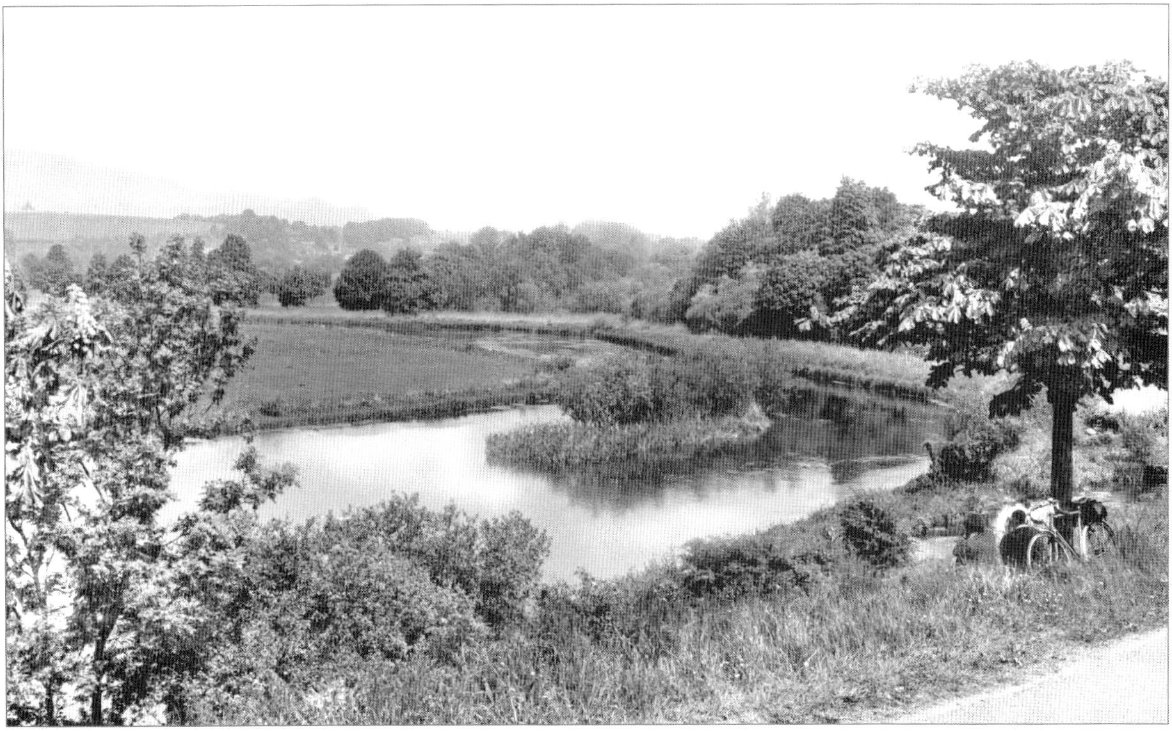

CHILBOLTON, *The River Test c1965* C227014

The perfect excursion: a cycle ride to a vantage point where the Test can be seen at its best. In the distance the rolling expanse of field and down is broken by dark woods and long strips of coppice, while nearer at hand the clear chalk streams broaden into wide shallow sweeps surrounding reedy islands with flowery borders and grey-green willows - pure delight.

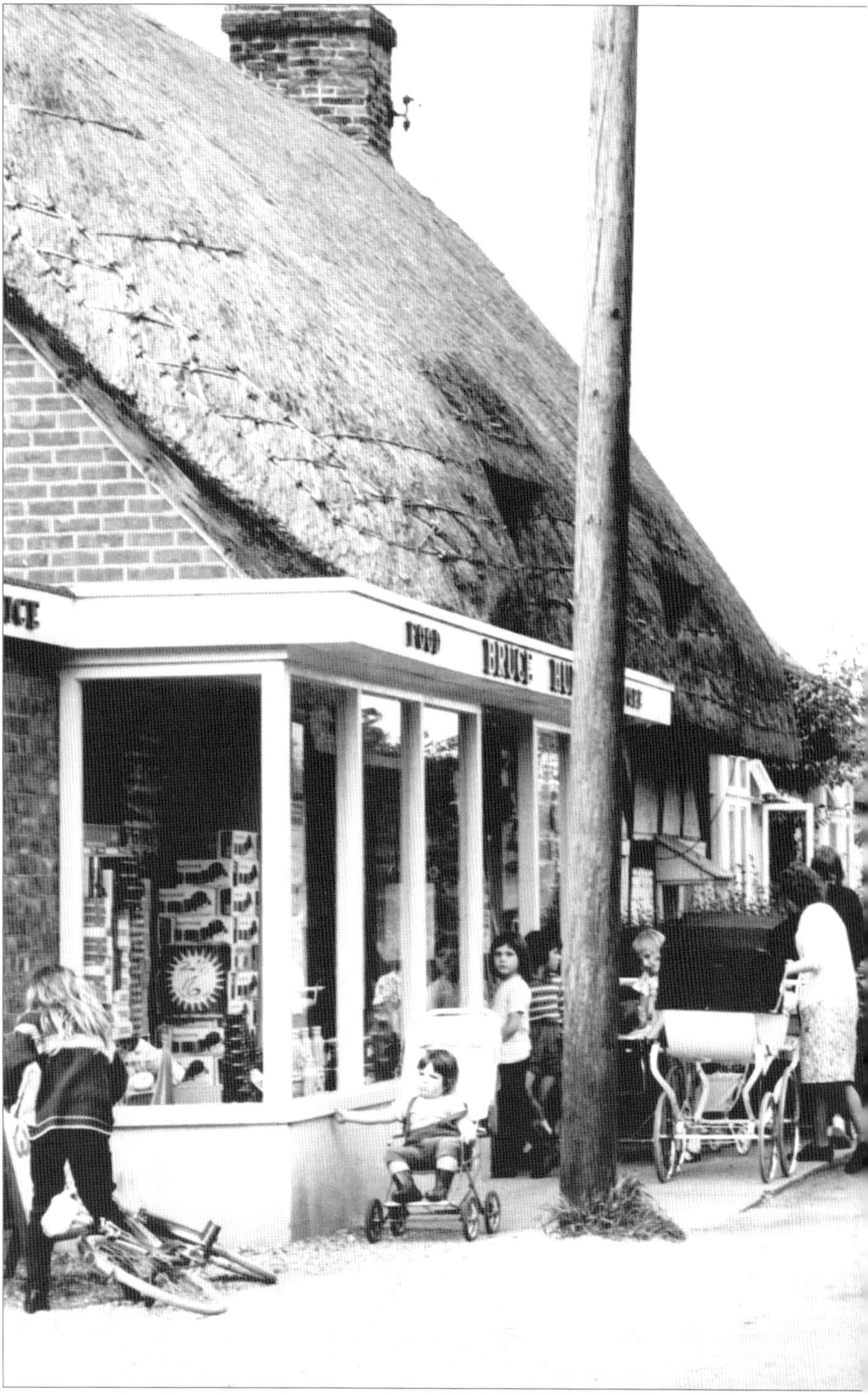

CHILBOLTON
High Street c1965 C227018

A true perambulation, as mothers and others wheel their way to the Post Office Stores at the end of the school day. Bruce Hunt's grocery is no doubt ready for this gentle rush hour invasion, and judging from the expectant faces of the children, it's the sweet counter that will draw most attention.

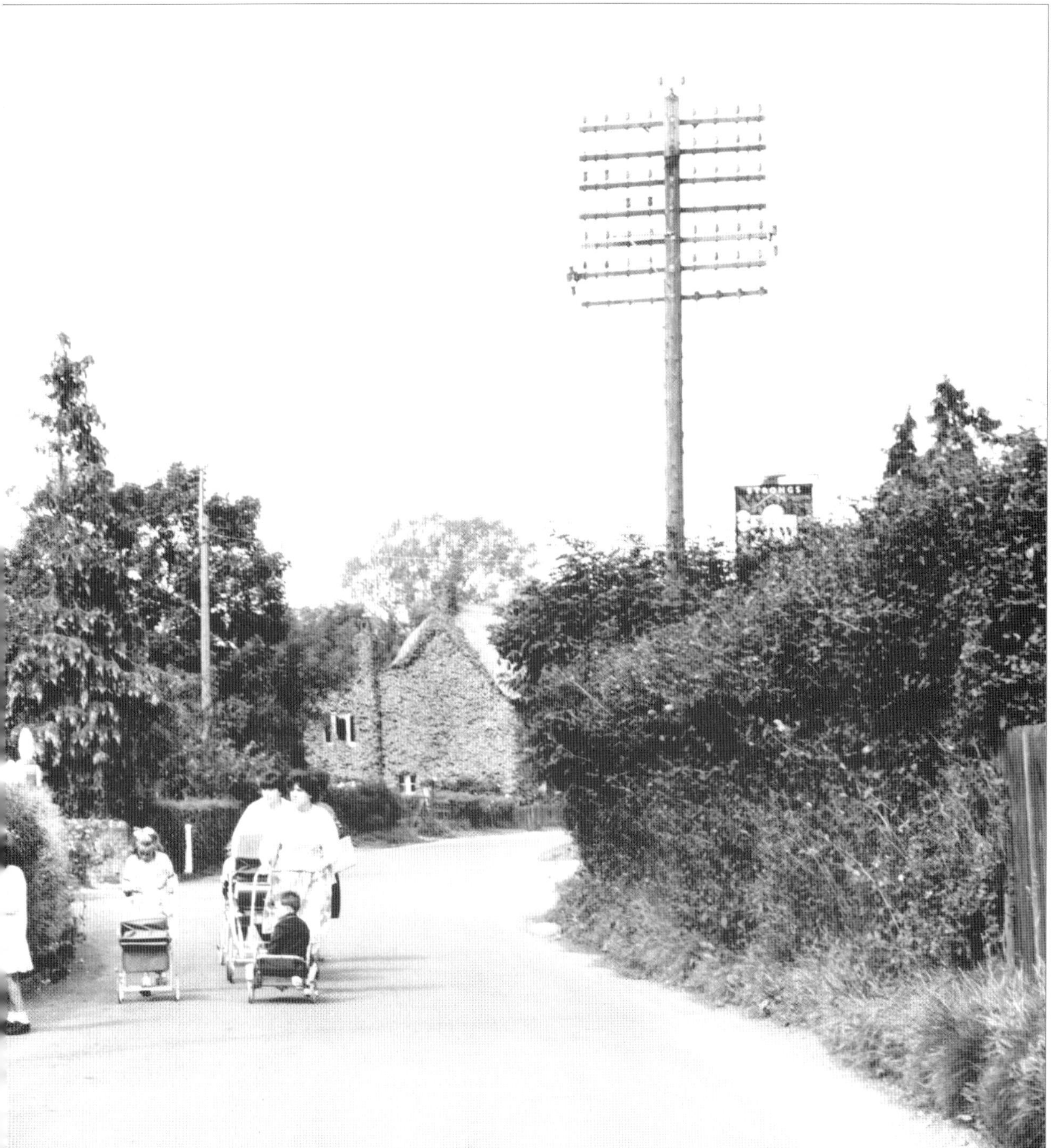
STRONGS

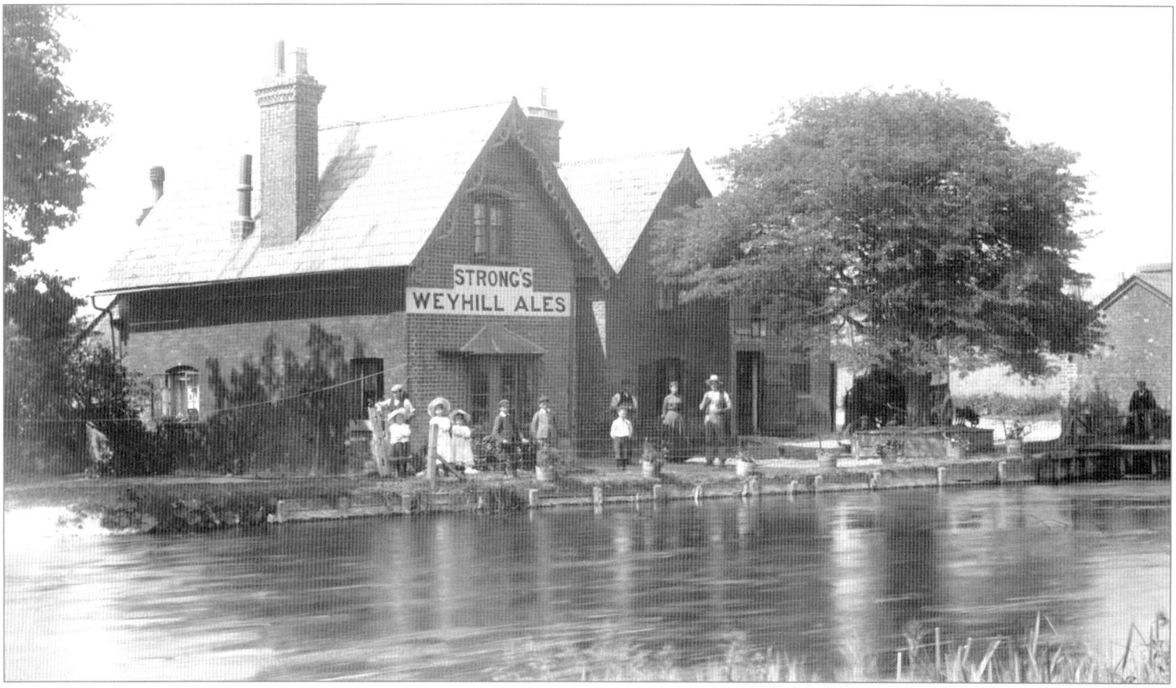

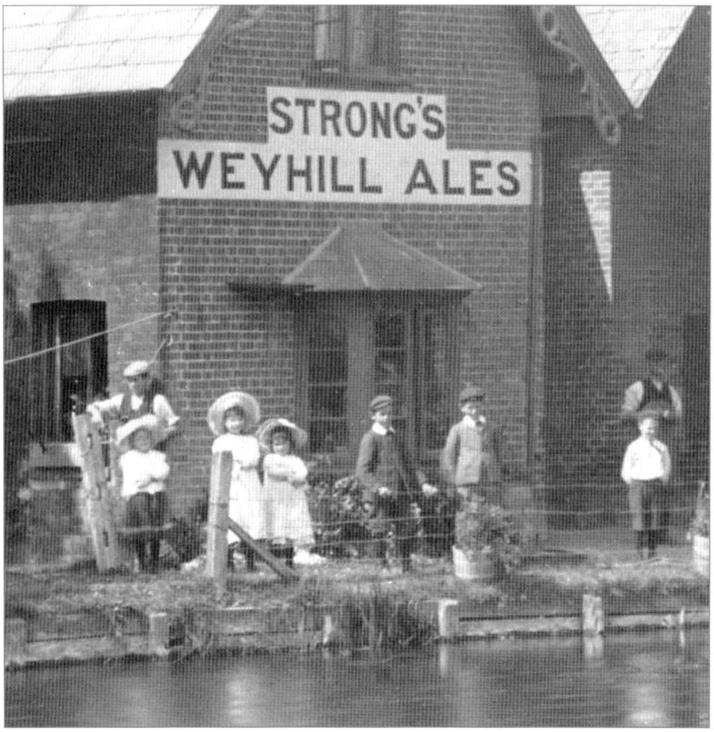

▲ **CHILBOLTON,** *Testcombe, The Seven Stars c1907* C227301

The Seven Stars public house (today the Mayfly) apparently began life as a lock keeper's cottage on the Redbridge to Andover canal (1796-1859). The canal company was bought out, and the cut was filled with chalk quarried nearby and replaced by a railway (1865-1974). The pub was in existence by 1880, and with its genial landlord Harry Nutley in charge, had a reputation for being a very convivial place. This group are certainly wreathed with smiles as they pose for the photographer, the children well dressed and well behaved as they stand behind the low fence that keeps them back from the water's edge.

◄ *detail from* C227301

FULLERTON
The Mill c1960 F109005

The village's name means 'wildfowlers' farm or hamlet', and is well suited to a location at the confluence of the Test, Dever and Anton. The brick-built mill and mill house are constructed in one continuous range, although the mill is mostly hidden behind the trees. Inside, the date 1851 is carved on a beam, while a breastshot wheel, still in use in the 1960s for driving a woodsaw, turns and churns the waters of the tailrace.

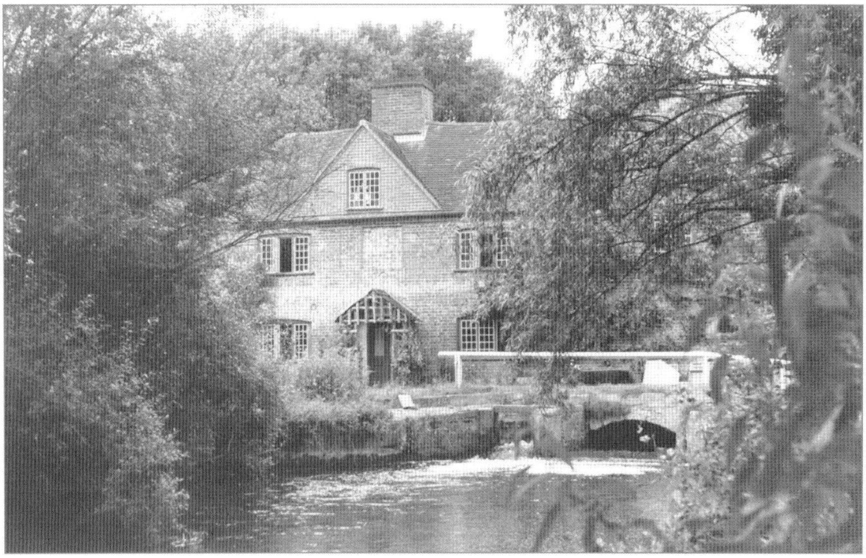

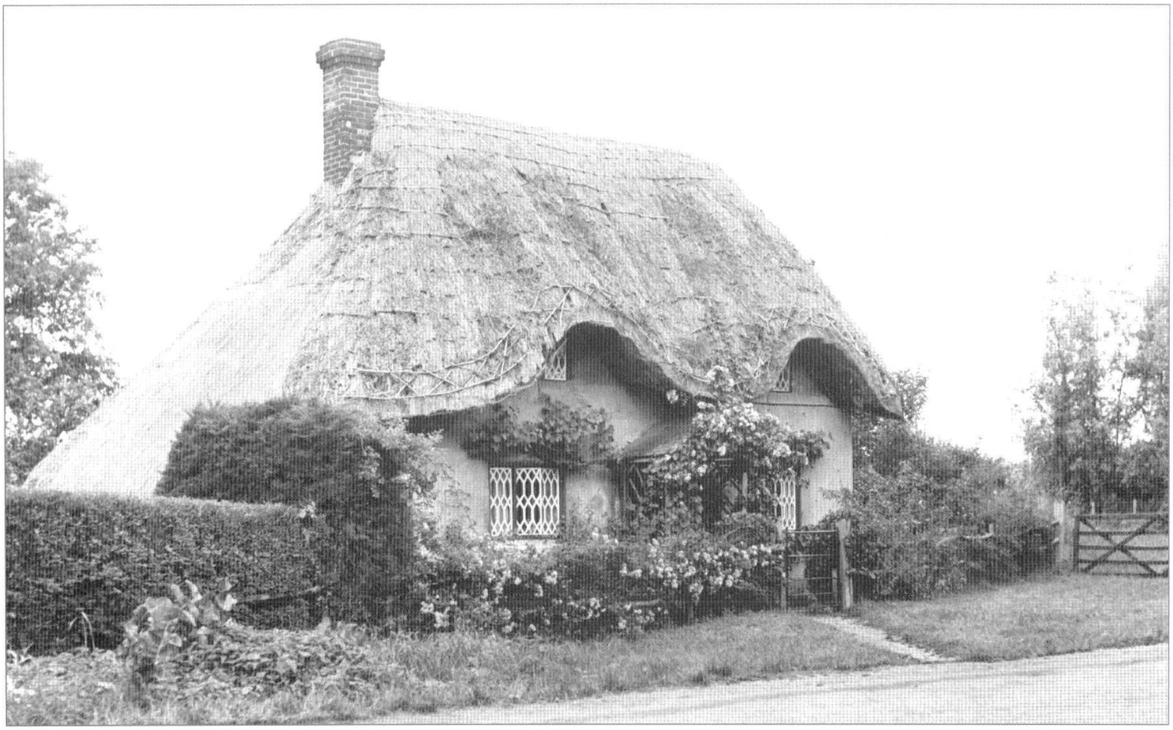

FULLERTON, *Vine Cottage c1960* F109004

This quintessential thatched cottage is made all the more attractive by the abundant blossoms that decorate the front boundary and rustic porch. The roof is raised over the two upper windows and brought down as a pentice, freshly thatched, to the left. The ornate windows are of 19th century date.

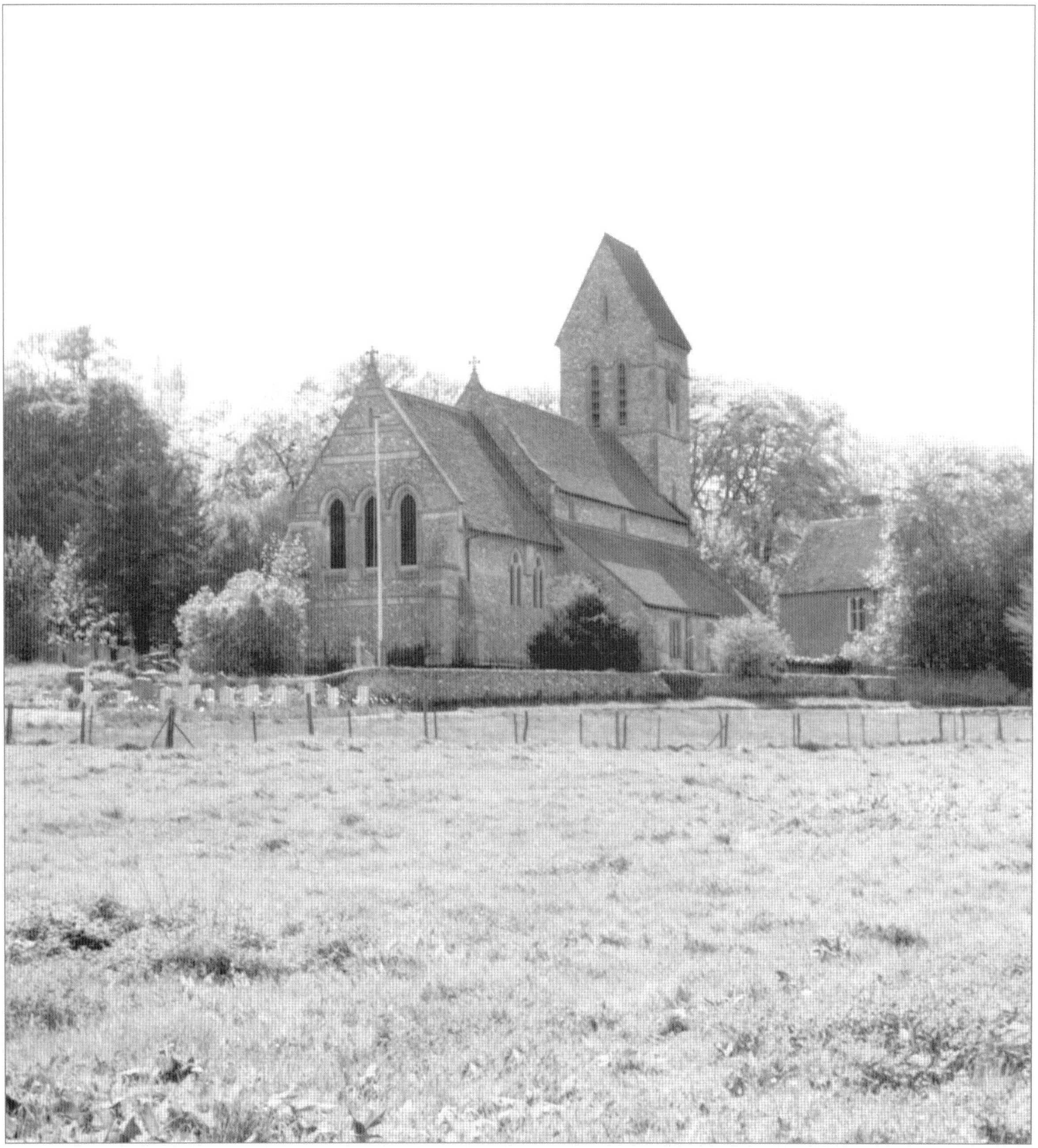

OVER WALLOP, *St Peter's Church c1965* O98025

J Pearson, the architect of Truro Cathedral, rebuilt this church in the mid 19th century. He designed the distinctive saddleback-style roof to the chancel and a plain west tower, which architectural historians describe as 'good'. Features of the 13th century were retained inside, and Pearson added touches of wrought iron, a material of which he was fond. In front of the church is a water meadow.

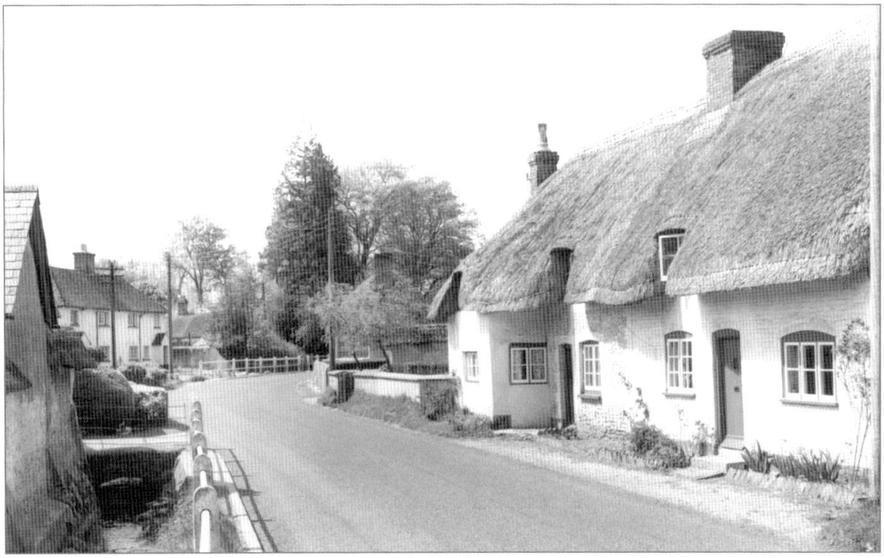

OVER WALLOP *Rose Cottage c1965* O98024

The Wallop Brook rises in Townsend field and flows beside Over Wallop's long village street. This street followed the north side of the stream, with railings to deter people from falling in and planks and handrails to access any properties to the south. The majority of dwellings were built on the north side of the road, presumably to catch the sunlight, as Rose Cottage is doing here.

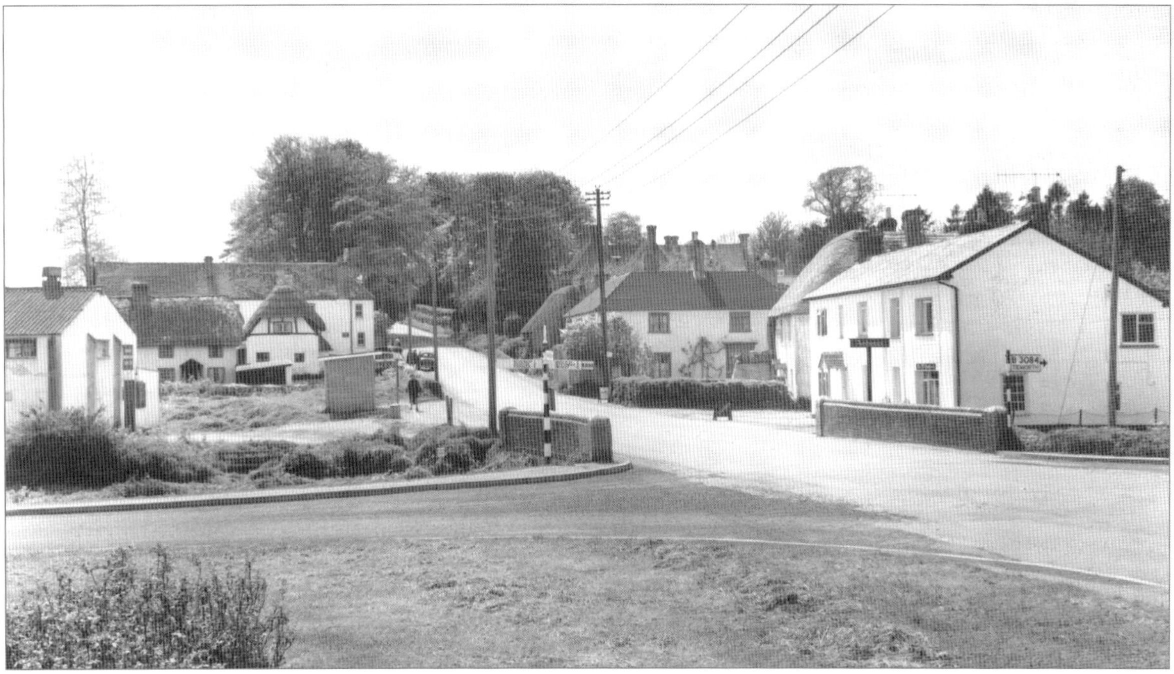

MIDDLE WALLOP, *The Crossroads c1965* M272017

This was a ford on the Andover to Salisbury turnpike, known locally as 'the lake' in winter, until 1857 when the Wallop Brook was bridged. The inhabitants then had to ward off summer dust from the chalk road with sheets of calico in their doorways, until the road was tarred. Road widening took place in 1931 and the first request for a speed limit came three years later. In this 1960s view all seems quiet. A solitary car is parked and a lone figure waits for a bus to Salisbury, while on the other side of the road, the café waits for custom.

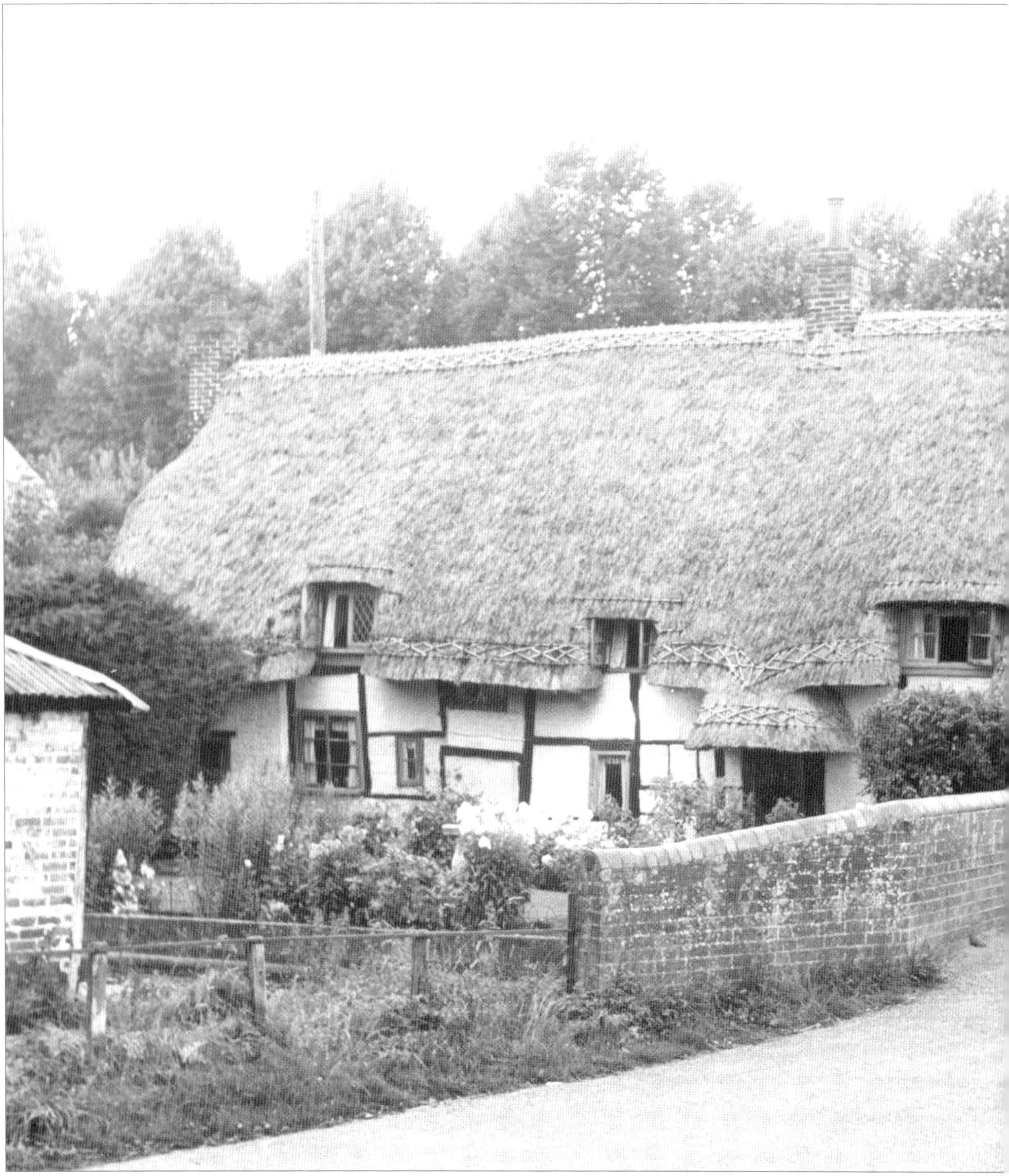

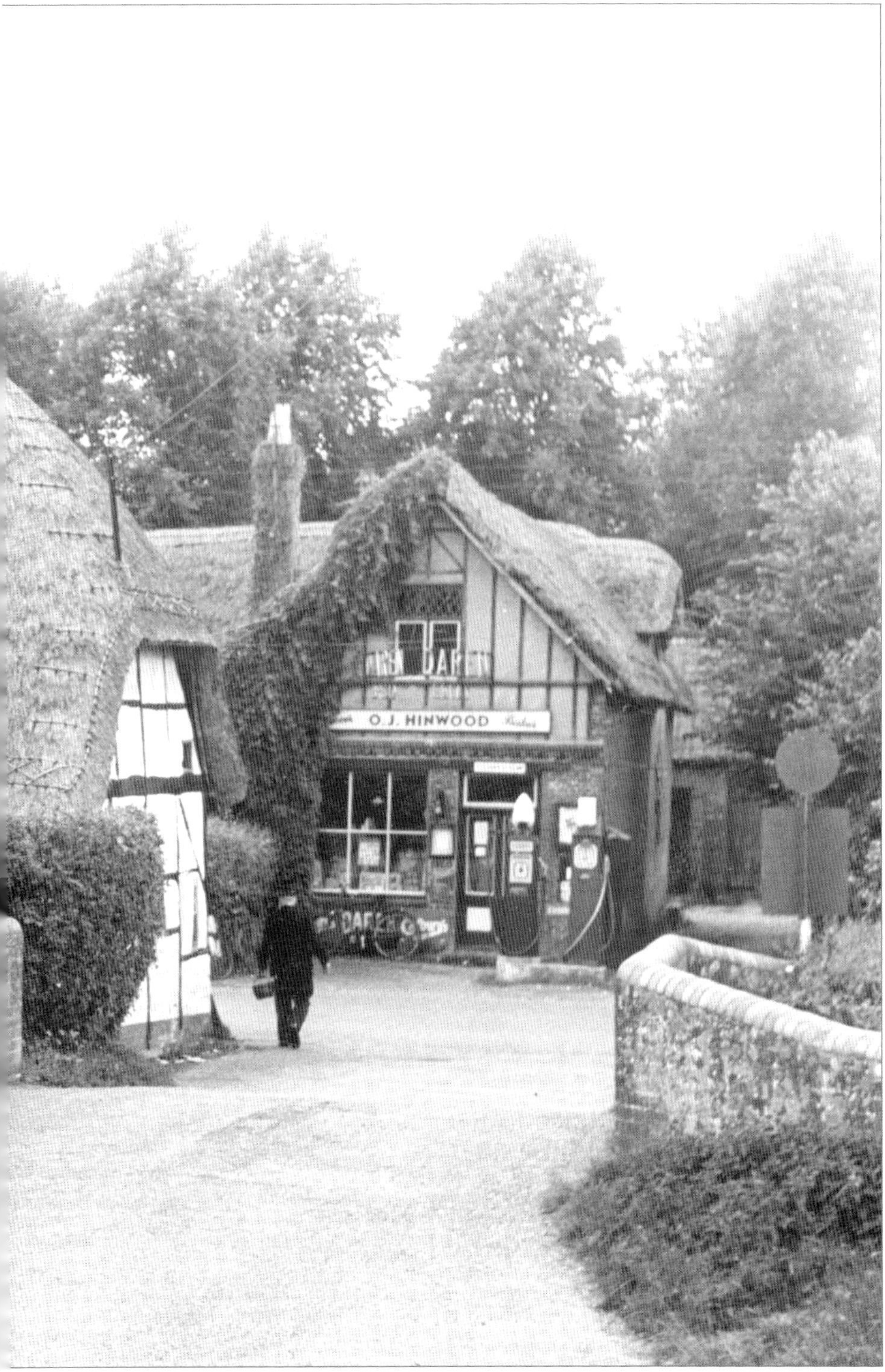

NETHER WALLOP
The Square
c1955 N156001

Nether Wallop is a large dense village with wandering streets full of thatched cottages. Mr Oliver Hinwood (his shop faces the photographer) served the villagers as postmaster from 1903 to 1961, as well as baking fresh bread daily, and supplying them with fuel. The gentleman walking past the cottage towards the shop was concerned with satisfying the spiritual needs of some of the community; he is the Reverend F W Hyne-Davy, vicar of St Andrew's.

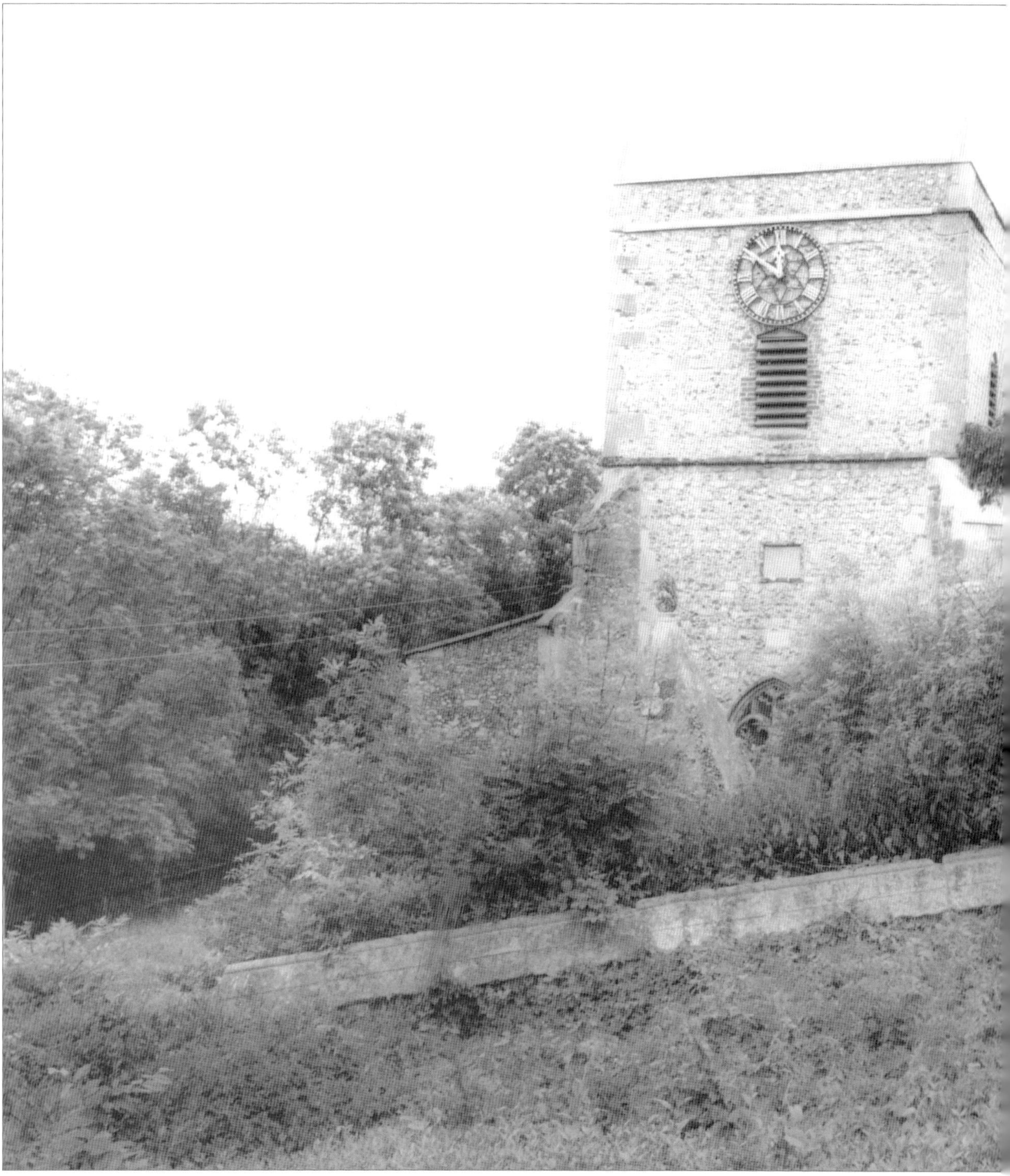

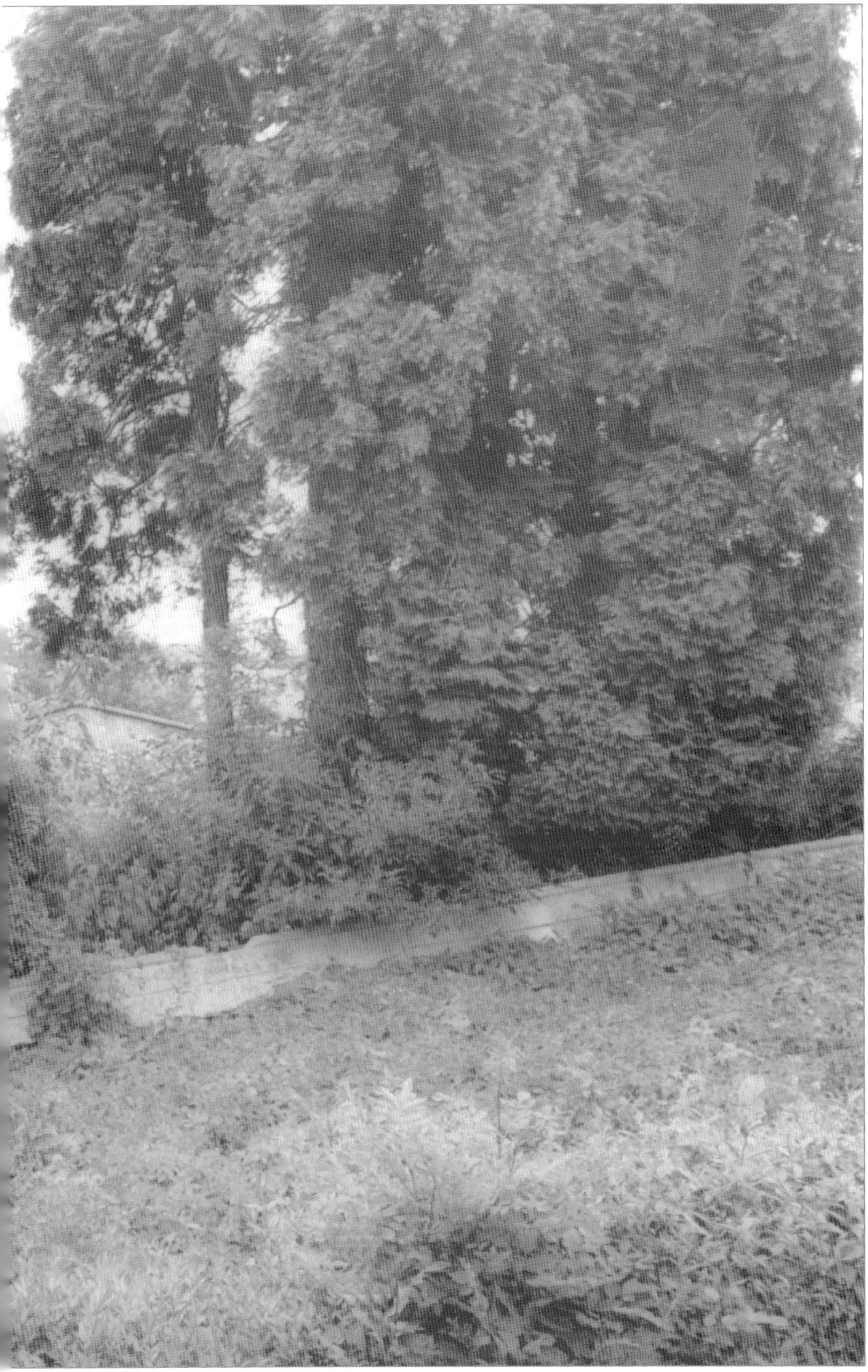

NETHER WALLOP
St Andrew's Church c1965 N156017

This late Anglo-Saxon church has been much altered, repaired, propped up and renewed over the centuries, part of the problem being the water that springs eternal beneath its foundations. The flint-built west tower dates from 1704 - the external brick facing and buttresses were added fifty years later. More recent work has been done; a small tablet states 'Tower restored 1959 - P J Mouland and Sons, Builders', and aluminium has been used in the roof to lessen the weight on the aged frame. The interior is complex. Just visible in front of the tower is the pyramidal mausoleum memorial to Dr Francis Douce, who died in 1760.

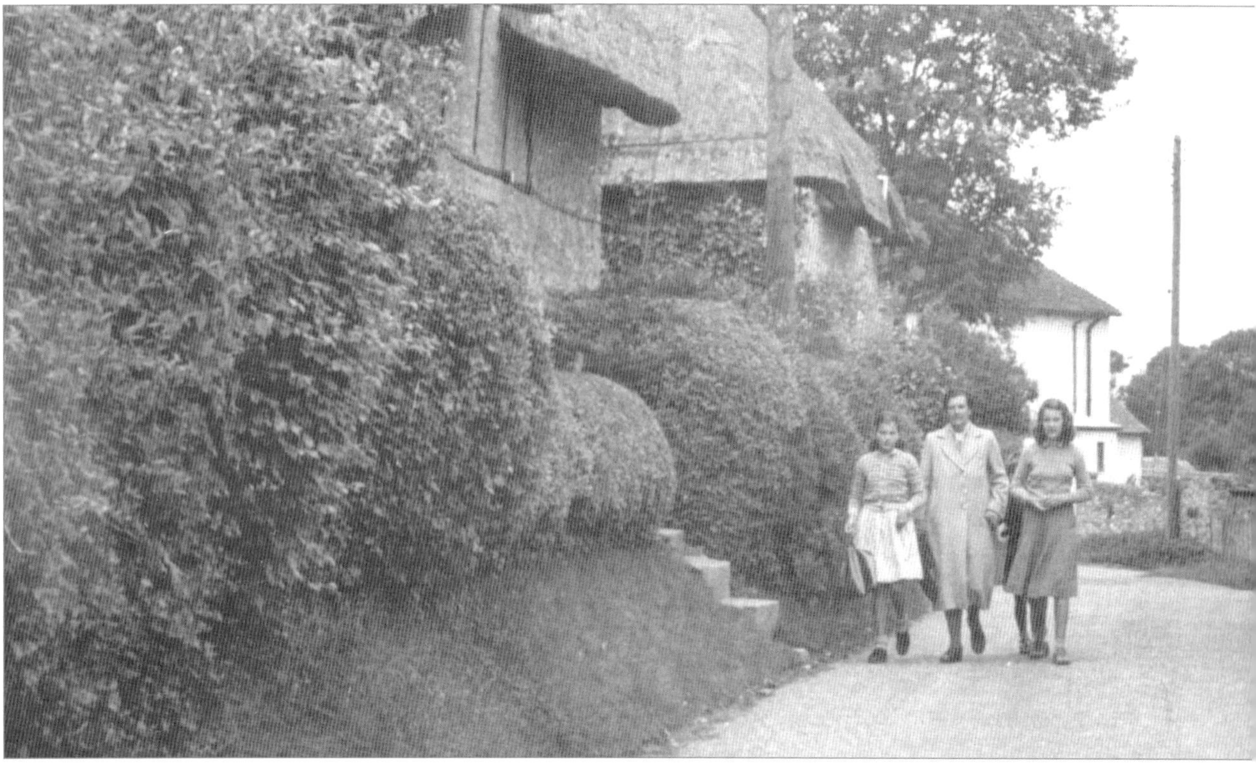

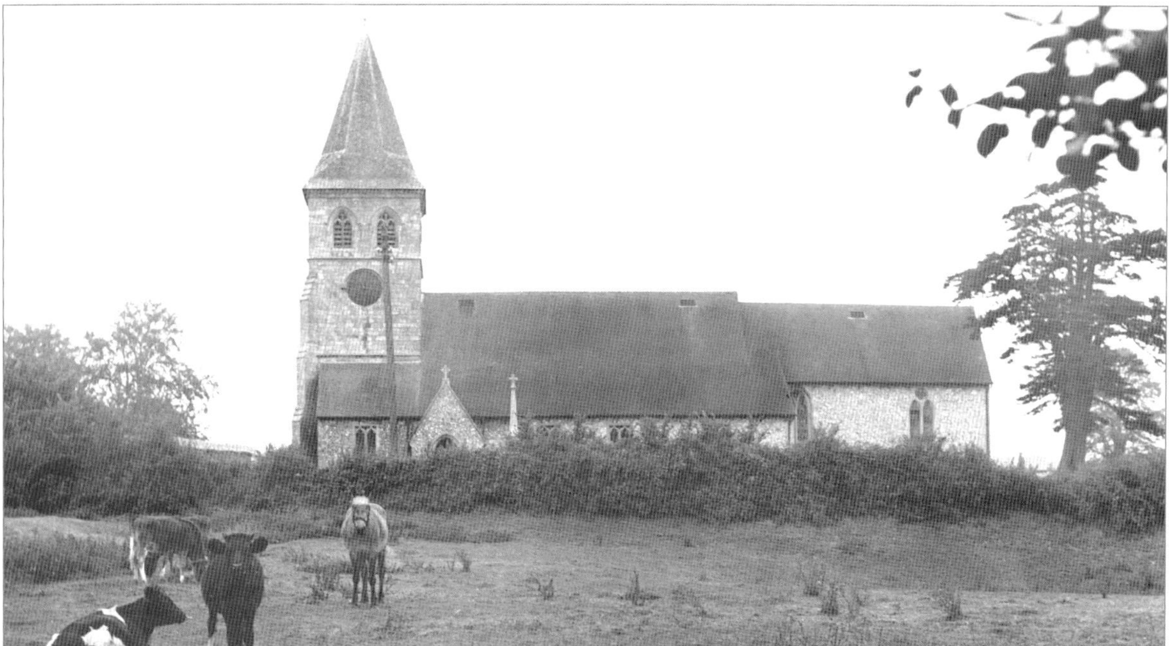

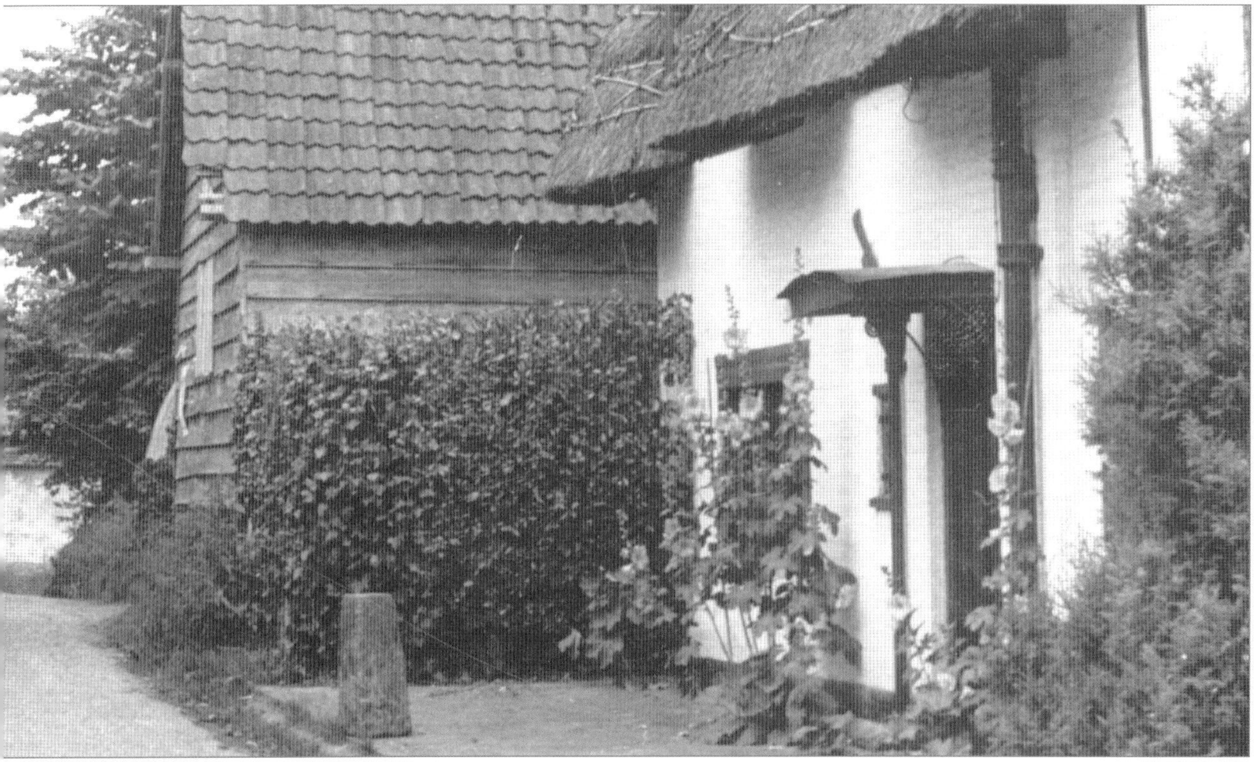

▲ **NETHER WALLOP,** *High Street c1960* N156011

Eyes fixed firmly on the photographer, a mother leads her brood along the High Street. The older cottages to her right are timber-framed with brick infill and a precipitous climb to the front door. A tiled timber barn and whitewashed brick cottage are opposite, with a solitary staddle stone making its mark.

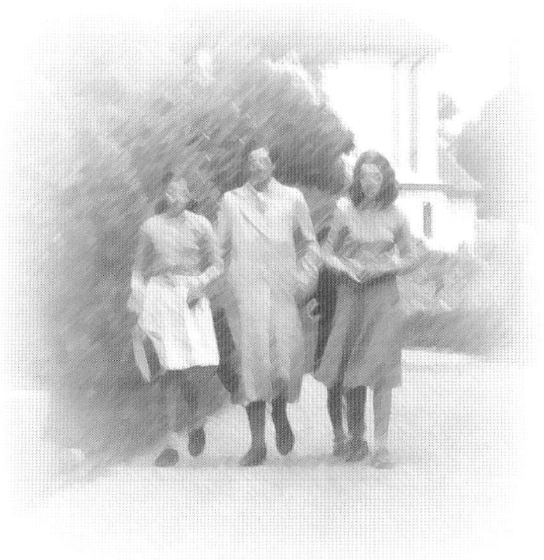

◄ **LONGSTOCK,** *The Church c1965* L578030

Longstock is a village full of thatched cottages, spread along the bank of the Test. This church is a 19th-century building (it was built between 1830 and 1837) and is described as being of 'no interest externally' by some. Nevertheless, the architect William White used 13th-century inspiration and mixed Early English and Decorated styles. He built in flint, and the tower is capped with an octagonal shingled broach spire. The chancel interior is 'exquisite'. The Longstock menagerie is impassive.

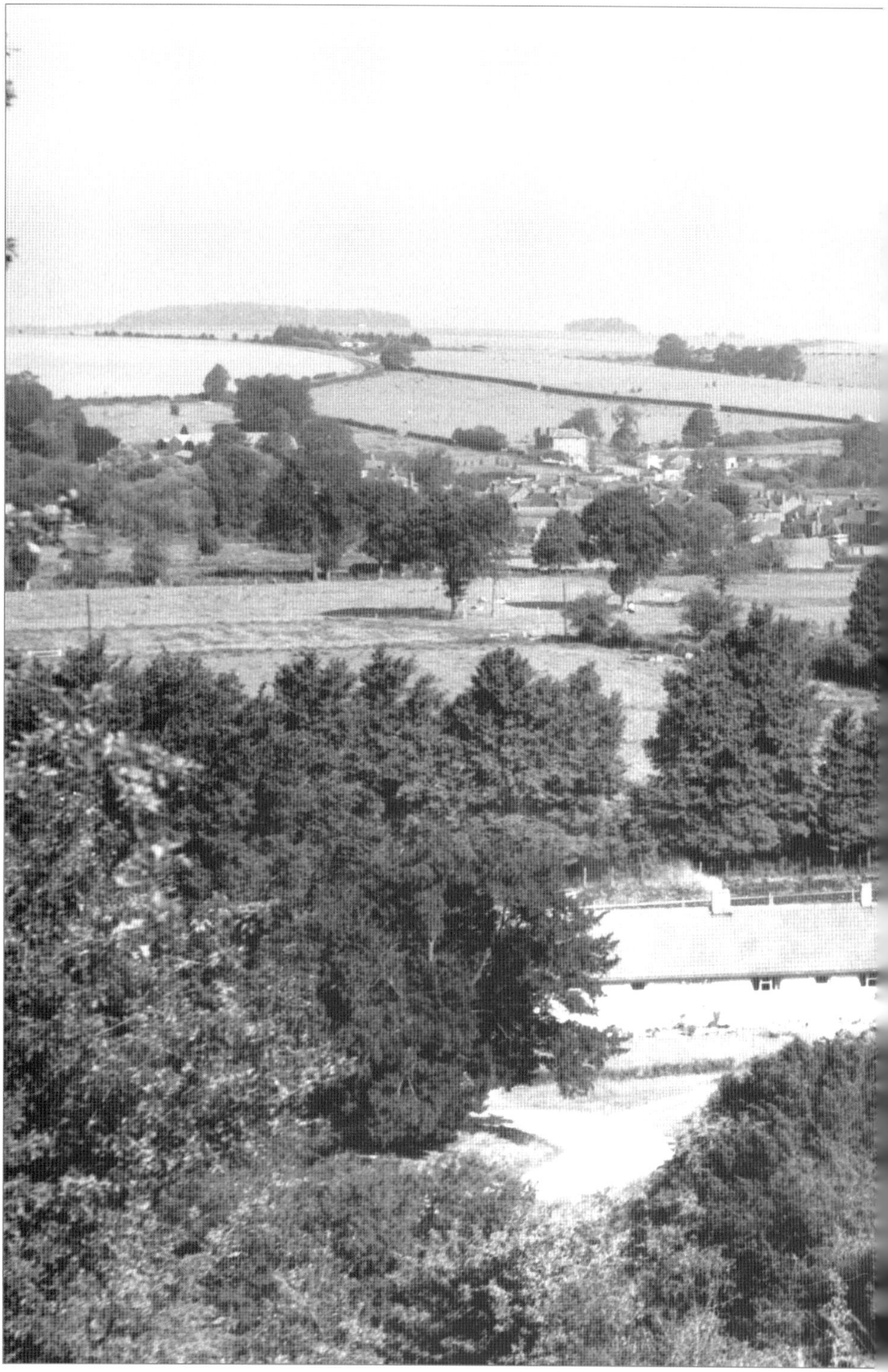

STOCKBRIDGE
The Test Valley
c1965 S259082

In this panoramic view of Stockbridge, Manor Farm occupies the foreground, with a glimpse of the Andover - Romsey railway, closed but not lifted, just beyond. Next come the broad fields leading to the Common Marsh. St Peter's provides a good marker for the town and points at Cleave Hill. More densely wooded Danebury is far to the left.

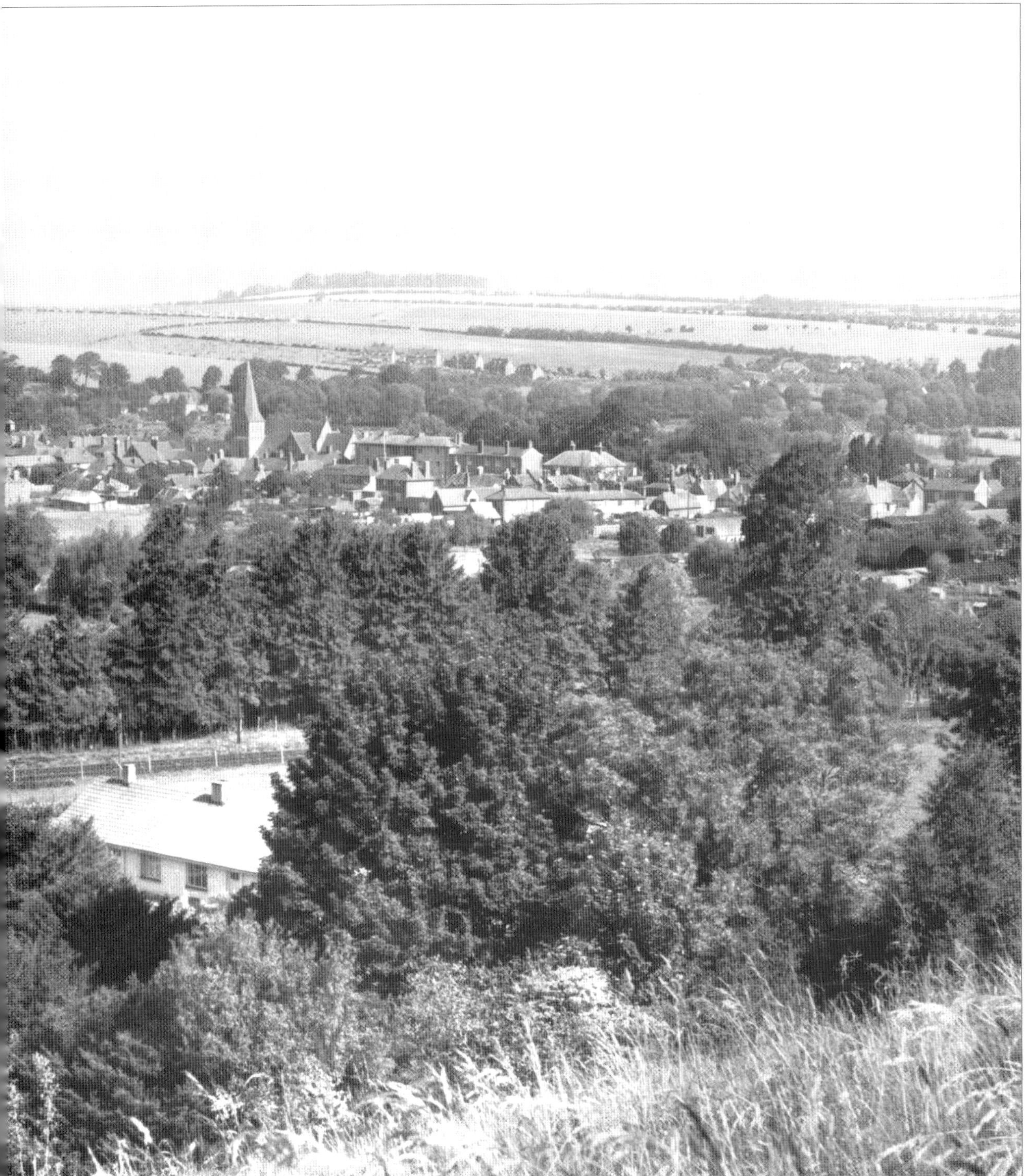

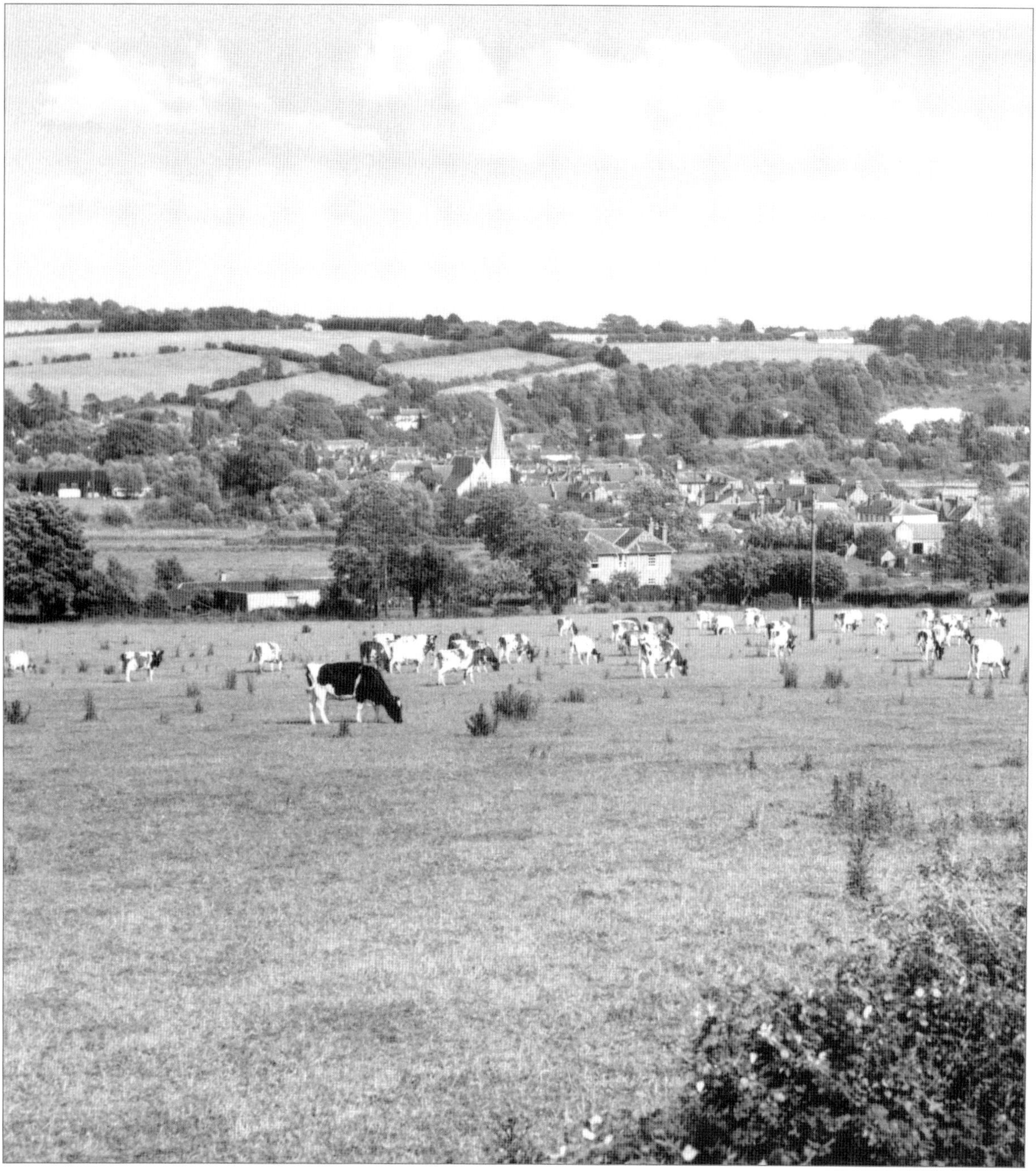

STOCKBRIDGE, *General View c1955* S259065

Two or three cattle pose, while the remainder concentrate on grazing, in this view of Stockbridge from the west. The confined nature of the village perched on its chalk causeway is quite apparent. St Peter's steeple just breaks the line of the Romsey road as it toils up the hill, with a chalk quarry visible below, and Steepleton House above.

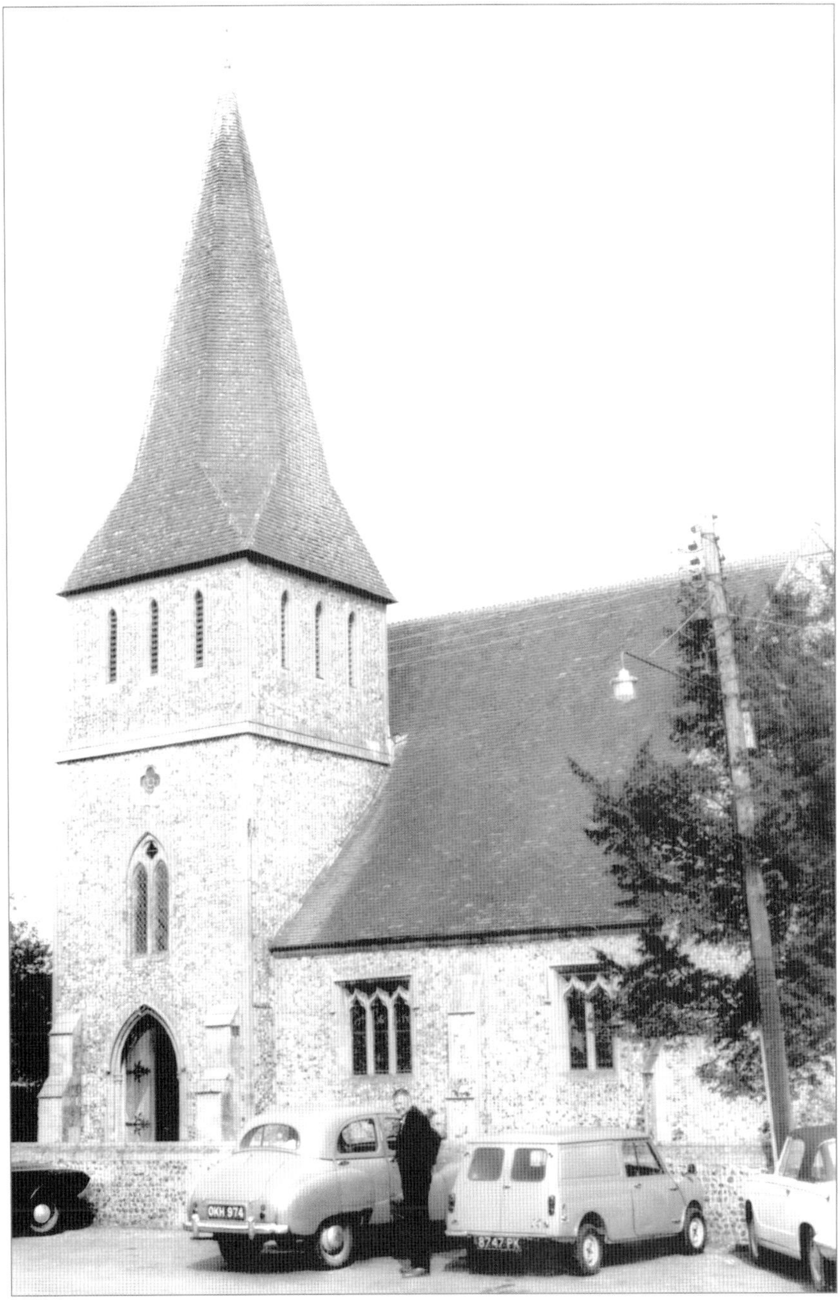

STOCKBRIDGE, *St Peter's Church c1965* S259099

The medieval St Peter's Chapel, on the eastern edge of the village, became a church in 1842, but twenty years later it was considered 'unfit for public worship'. In 1866 a new Victorian Gothic-style church was built by the Winchester architect J Colson; the steeple was added in 1887. Elements of the old church were reused, and to save money the villagers trundled them down the High Street in wheelbarrows.

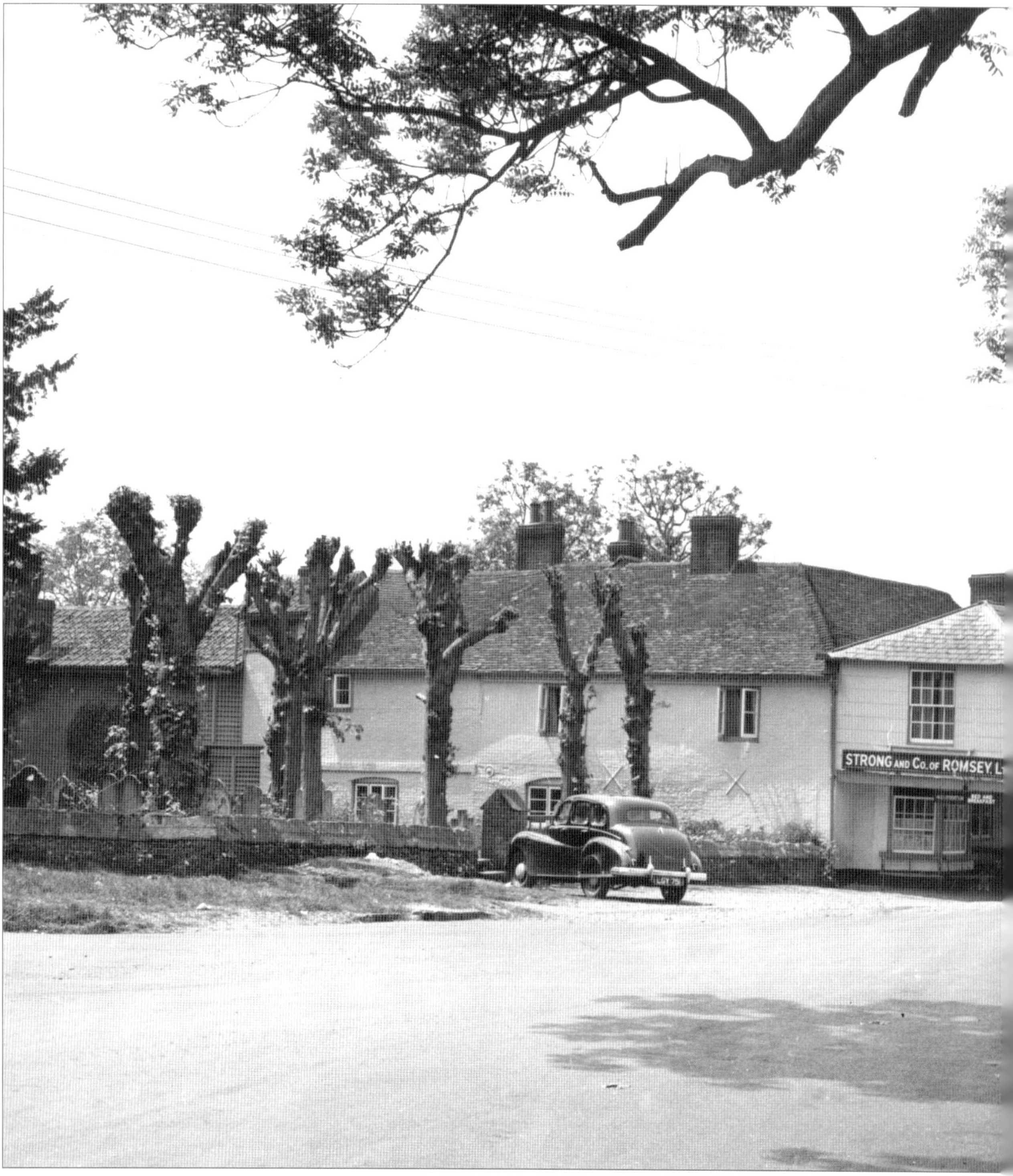
STRONG AND Co. OF ROMSEY, L

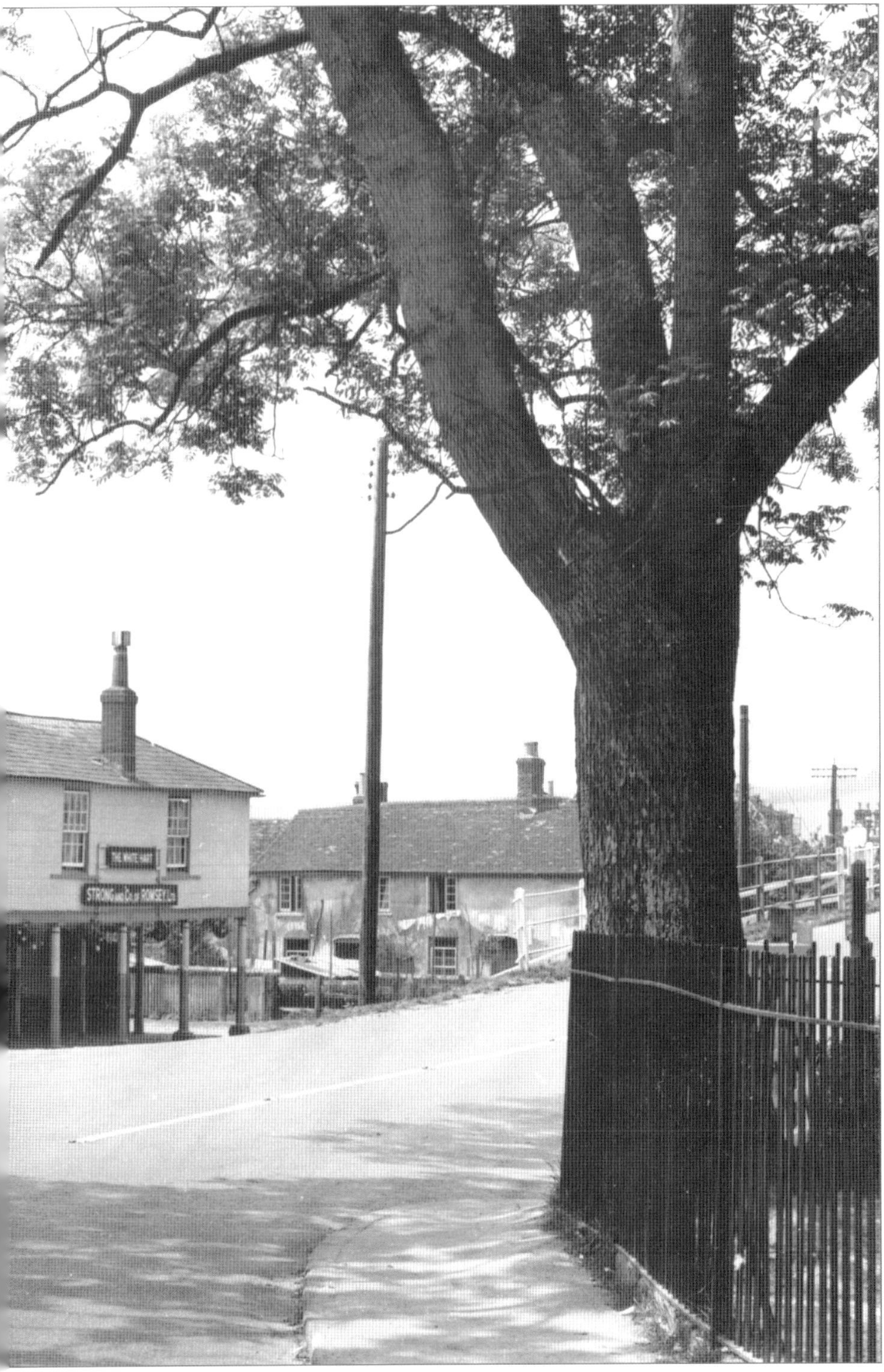

STOCKBRIDGE
The White Hart
c1955 S259051

In 1900 there were 13 pubs and inns in Stockbridge; today there are just five. The White Hart is one of the survivors. In this mid-century view it stands sentinel at the eastern approach to the village between the old churchyard, with its heavily pruned trees, and the railway. The building is clearly of mixed origins, with an older section with timber framing and tiled roof. To impress the potential customer a first-floor addition, balanced on five thin Tuscan style cast-iron columns with slate hung roof and walls, has been tacked onto the front. At this particular date, Strong & Co of Romsey provided the beverages.

STOCKBRIDGE
The View from the Bridge c1955 S259017

Stockbridge consists of a single wide street crossing the valley, with five or six bridges over strands of the river. Here, the bridge in question, which is affording a cyclist a fine bit of freewheeling, crossed the railway at the east end of the High Street. The Andover to Redbridge Railway opened in 1865 along the old course of the Andover canal, and Stockbridge had a substantial station to the right of this view. The line closed in 1964.

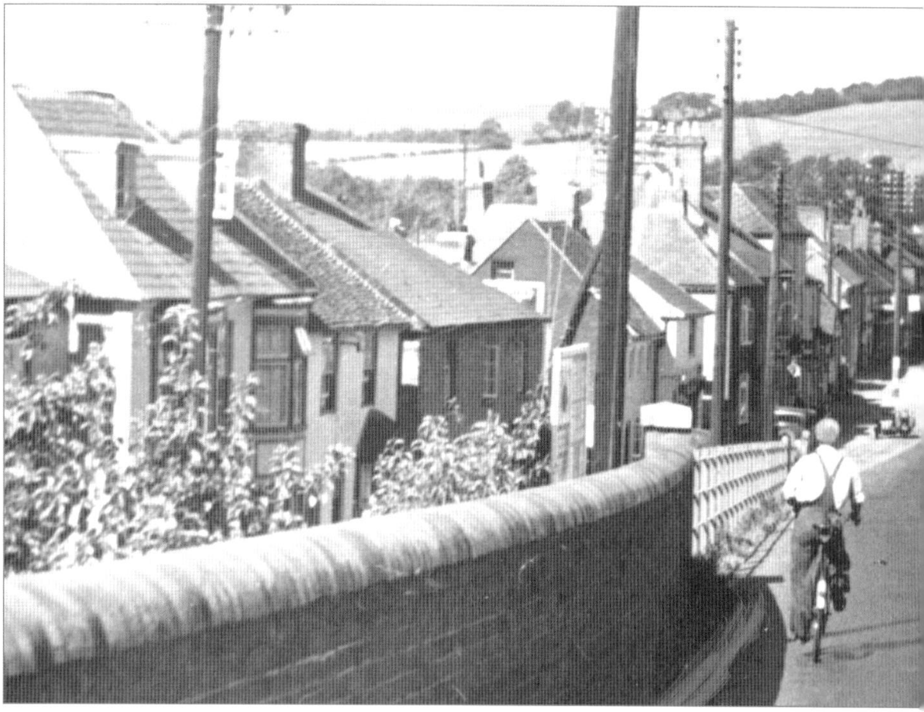

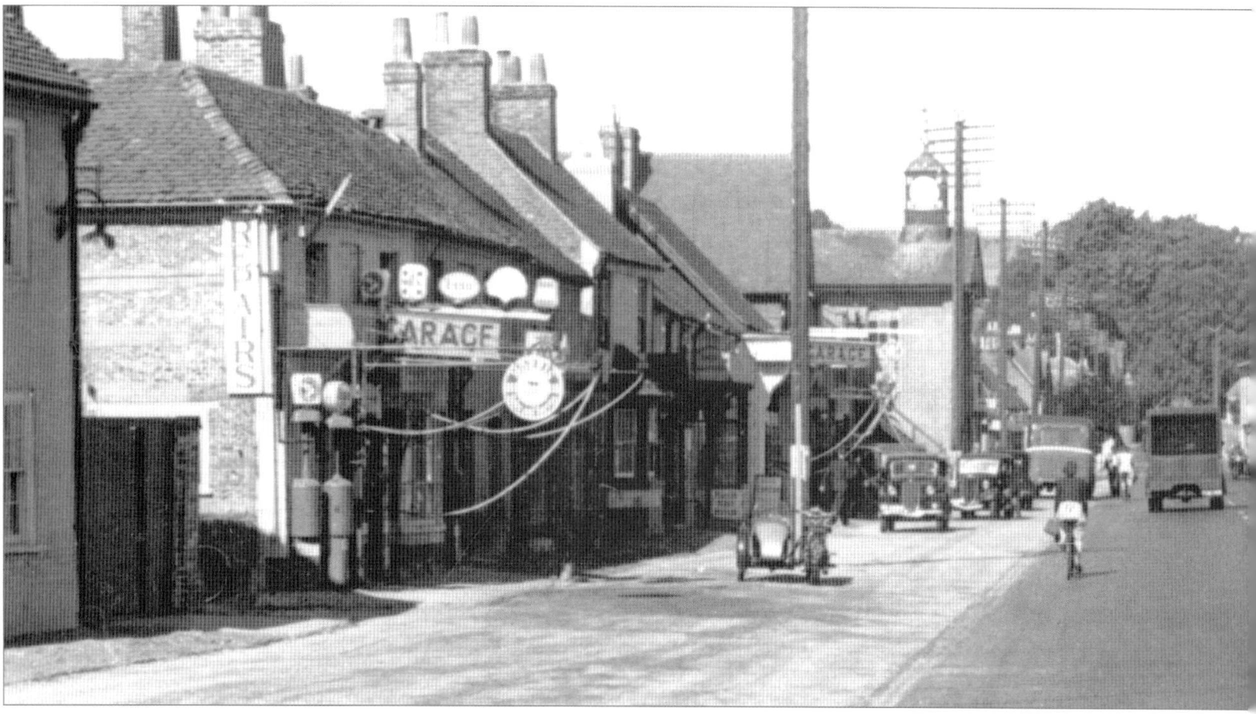

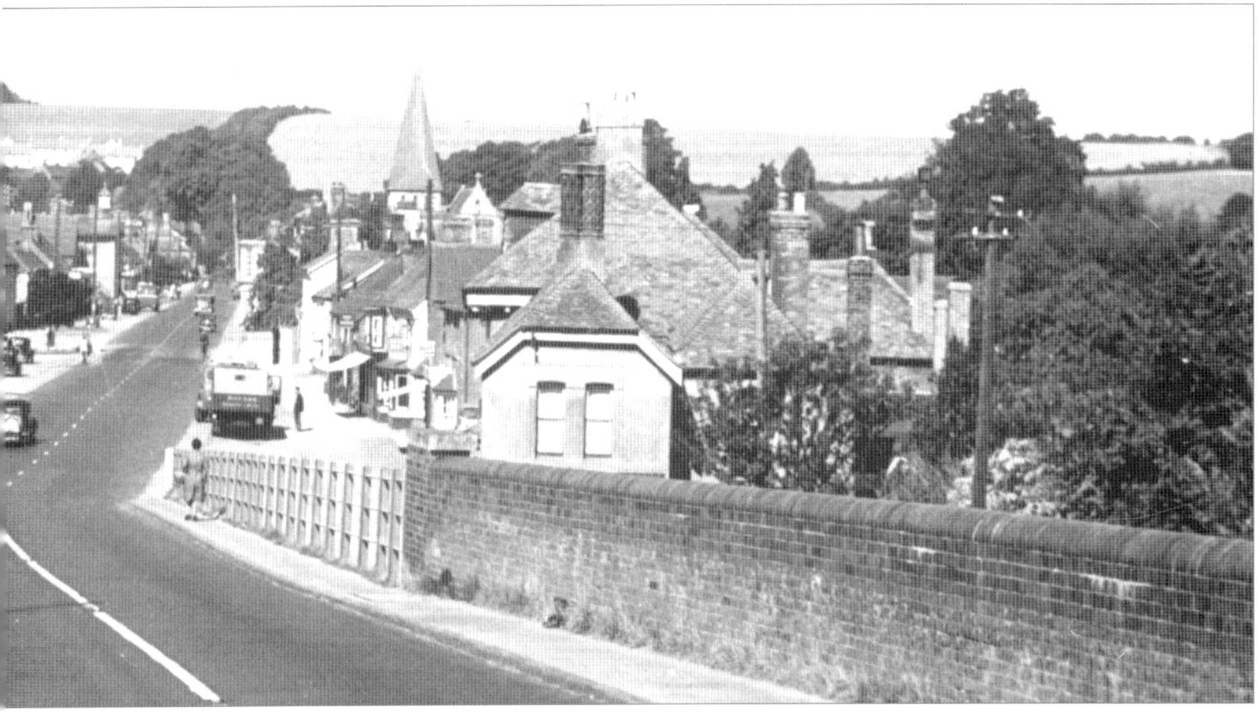

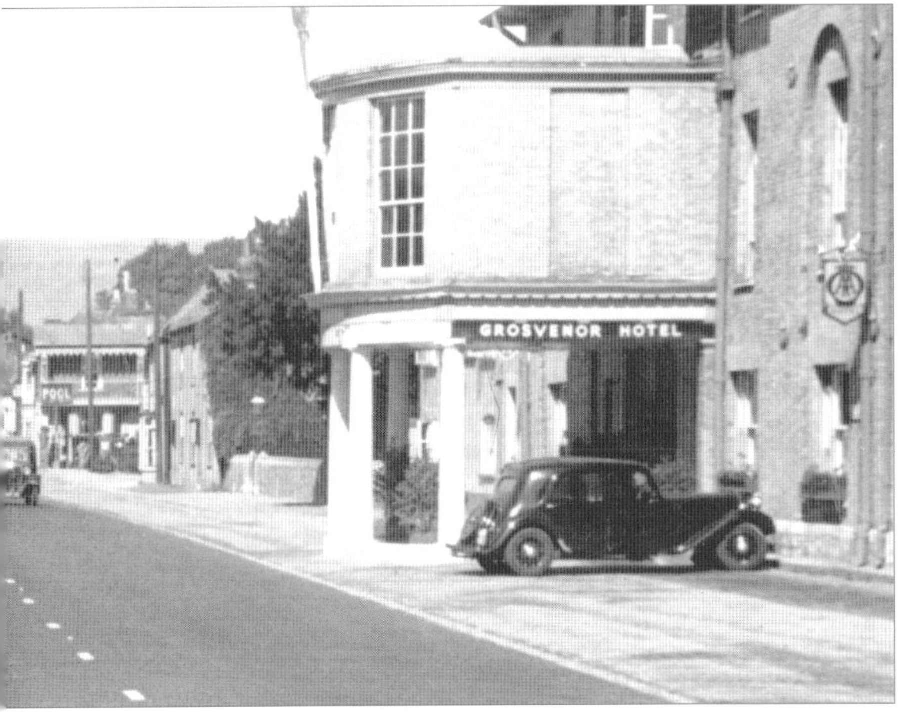

◄ **STOCKBRIDGE**
High Street c1955 S259019

Three garages, two on the left, including Fenning's, and Stoke's in the distance on the right, stand ready to dispense fuel from their elaborate booms, but the most eye-catching feature of this view is the yellow brick portico of the Grosvenor Hotel. The hotel, named after Lord Grosvenor, one-time MP, was built in 1790 on the site of the King's Head Inn. Former owners include Tom Cannon of Danebury Races fame. Today it belongs to the Houghton Fishing Club, founded in 1822 and probably the oldest dry fly fishing club in the world. The porch room, supported on its curved Doric colonnade, is its headquarters.

AN ORDNANCE SURVEY MAP SHOWING STOCKBRIDGE AND SURROUNDING AREAS *1894*

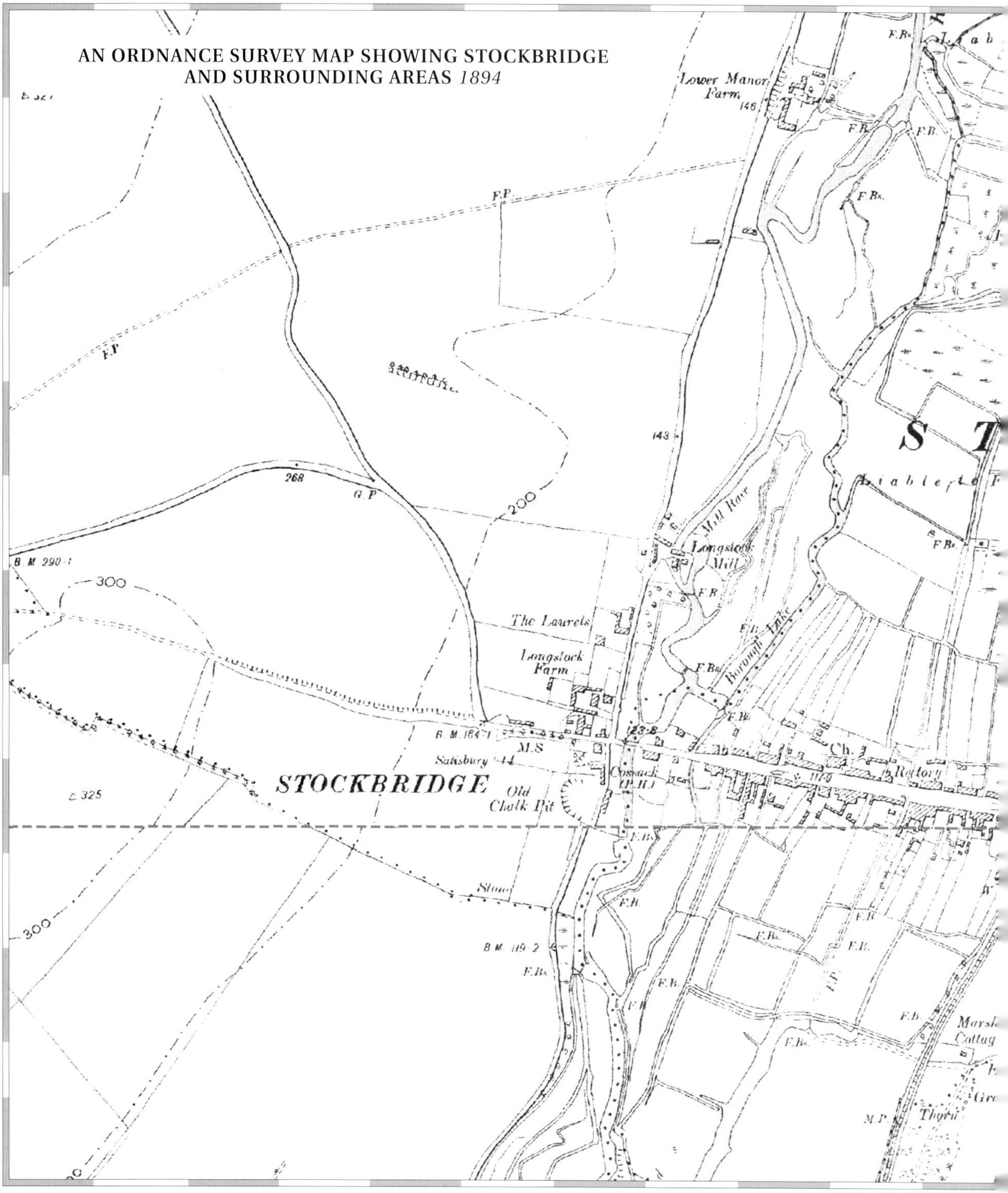

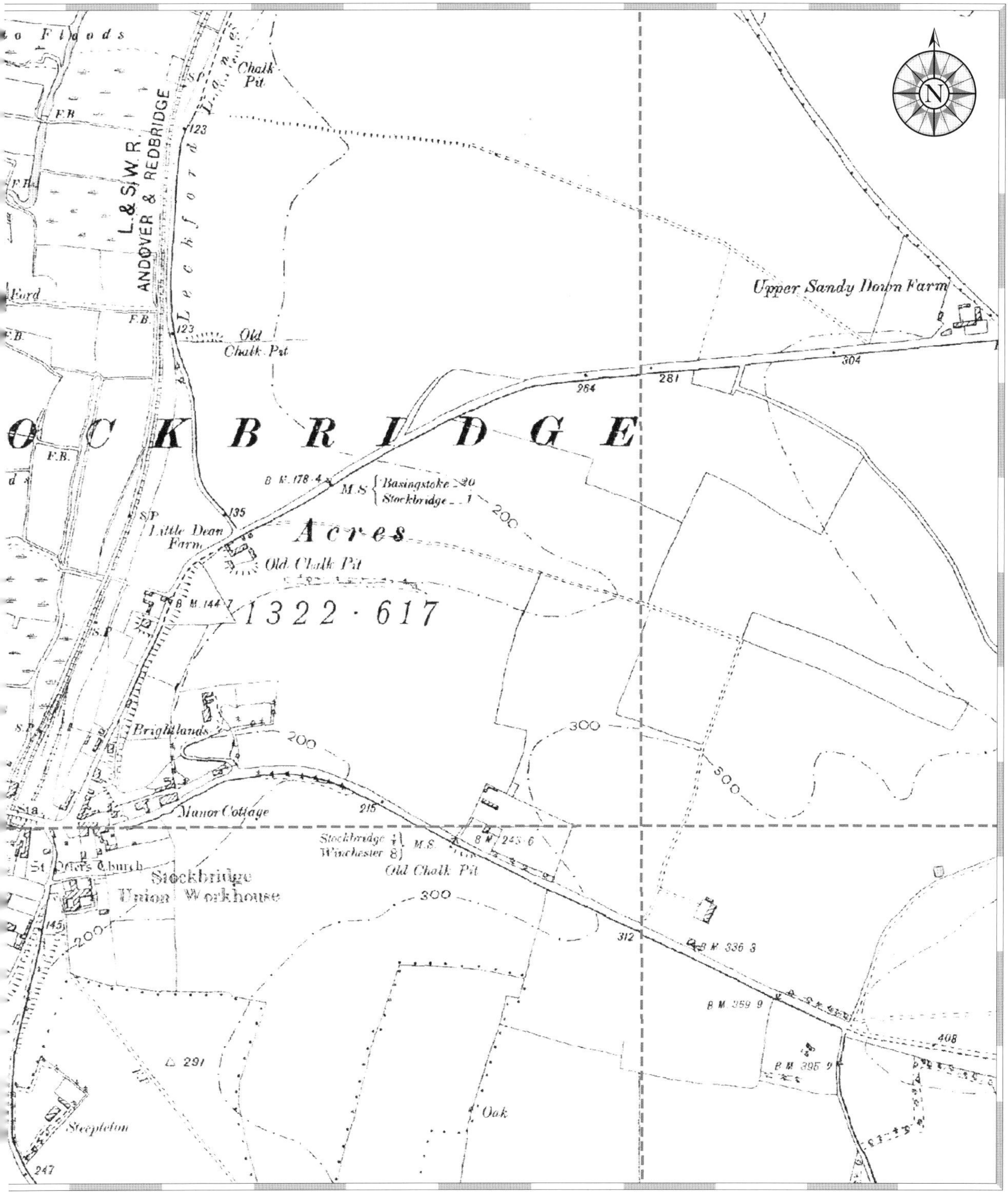
L. & S. W. R.
ANDOVER & REDBRIDGE
Chalk Pit
Old Chalk Pit
Upper Sandy Down Farm
OCKBRIDGE
Acres
1322·617
Little Dean Farm
Old Chalk Pit
Brightlands
Manor Cottage
St Peter's Church
Stockbridge Union Workhouse
Old Chalk Pit
Steepleton
Oak
300
200
500

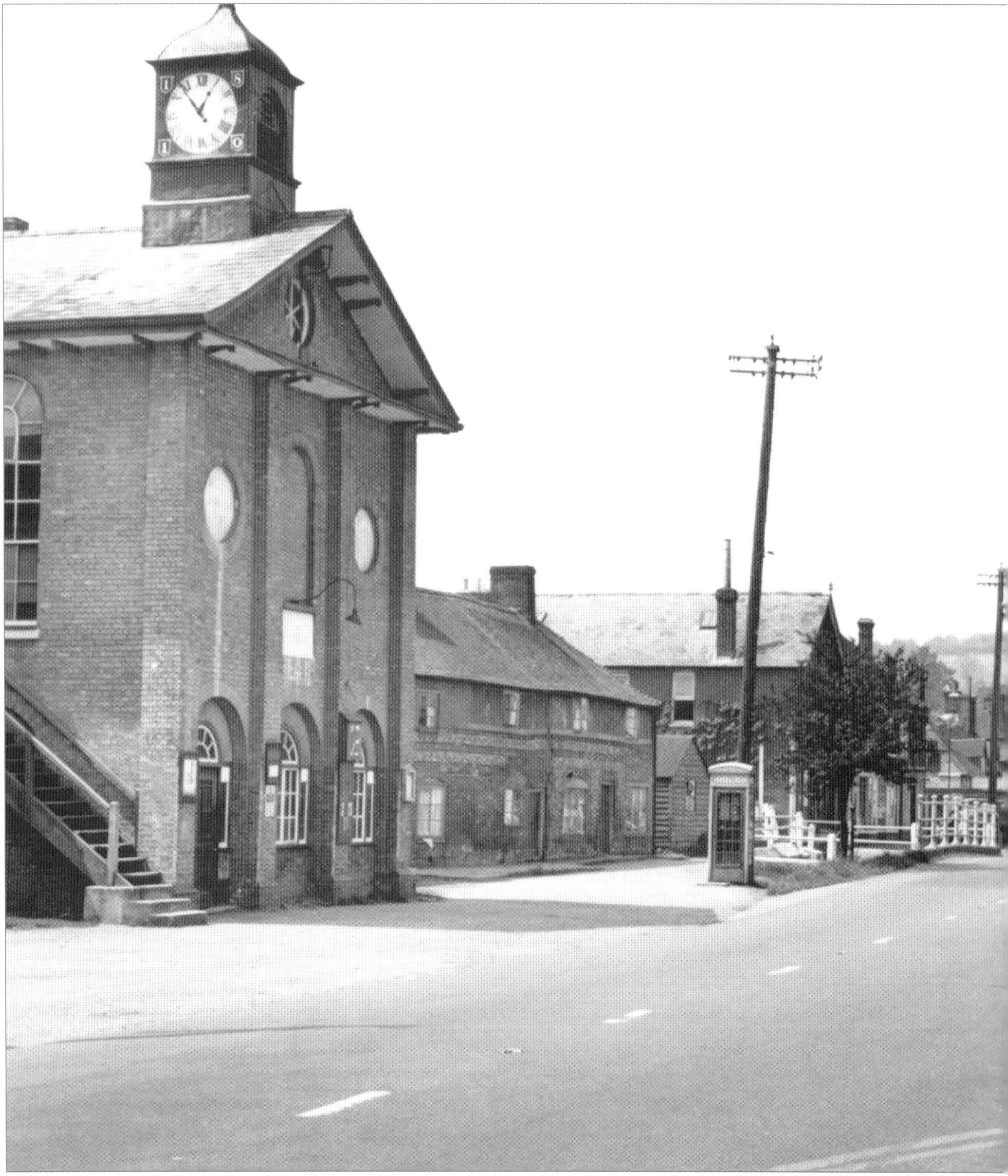

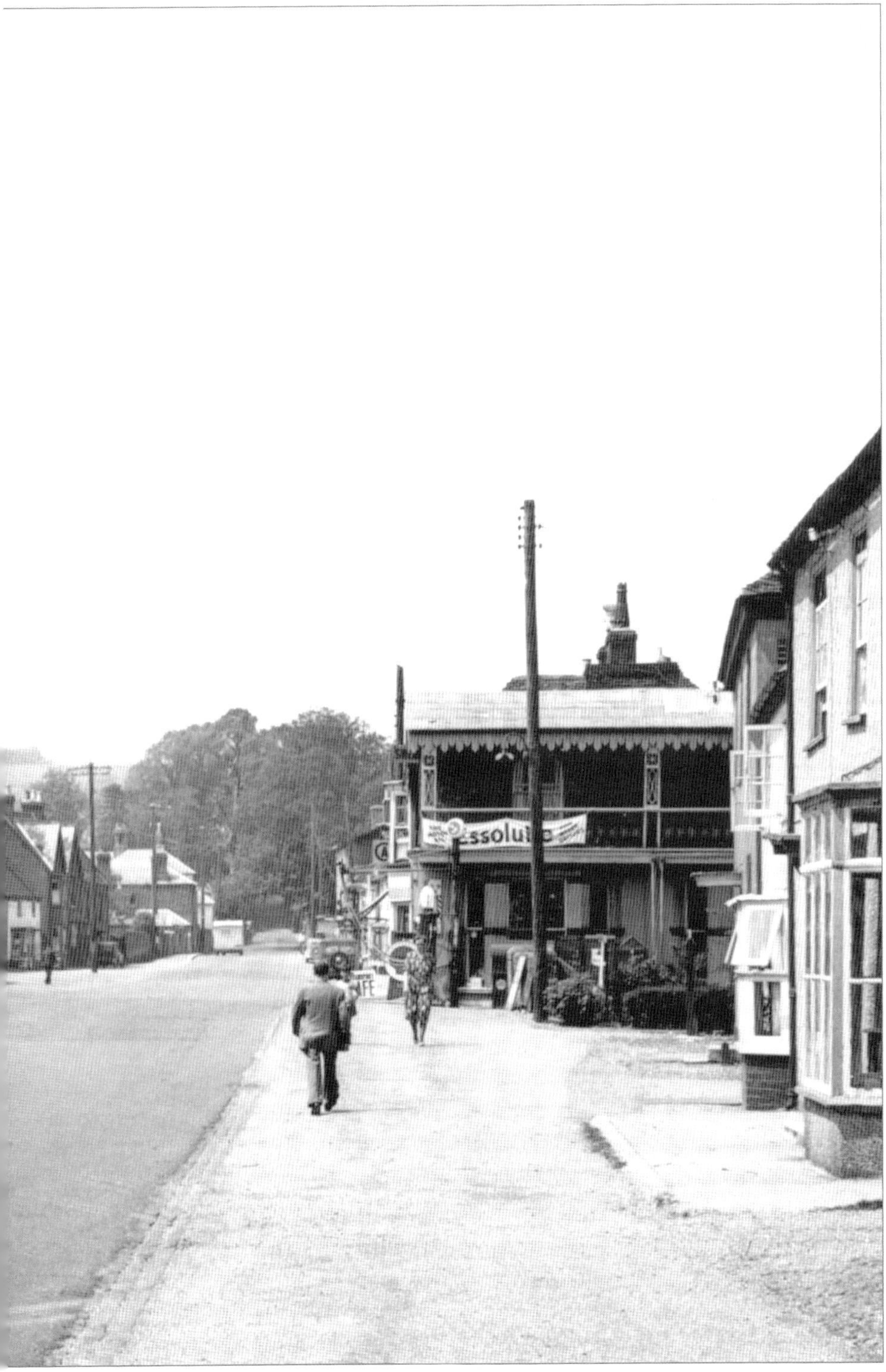

STOCKBRIDGE
High Street
c1955 S259049

Dominating the left side of this view is the Town Hall, built of yellow brick in 1790 by George Porter and Joseph Foster Barham as a 'rotten borough' election bribe. The clock was added four years later. The deep eaves provided some shelter for those below, but in 1810 the open arches were filled in, which accounts for the inscription 'AD 1810 - E Cooper, Bailiff' on the large plaque. On the right is Stoke's Garage, advertising Essolube. This ornate building of the late 19th century was inspired by a visit to Italy; it has a balcony from which processions associated with Danebury Races could be viewed.

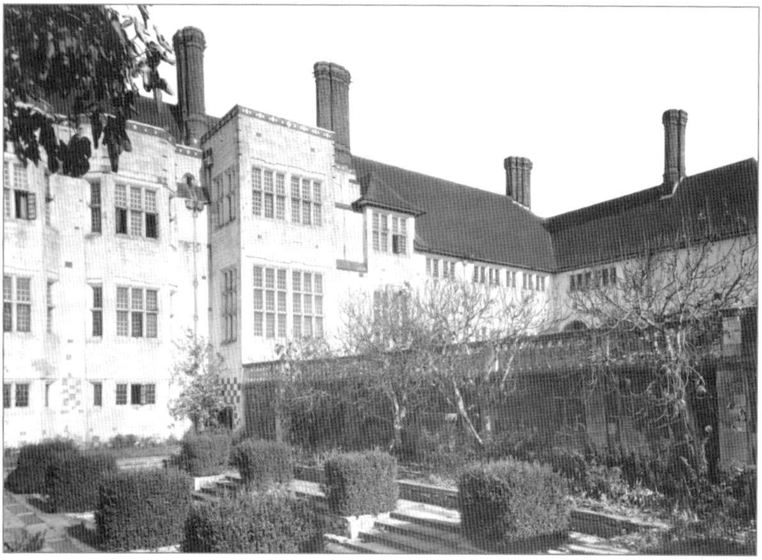

STOCKBRIDGE, *Marsh Court School 1951* S259057

Marsh Court, a huge white house constructed from chalk, was built by Sir Edwin Lutyens between 1901 and 1904 for Herbert Johnson, adventurer, stockbroker and sportsman. Lutyens also added a ballroom in 1926 so that Johnson, joint master of the Hursley Hunt, could host the hunt balls himself. The structure is of chalk ashlar with pieces of flint and tile, with mullioned and transom windows and a hipped tile roof. The north front has a symmetrical 'E' formation, but the south, seen here, provides a strong contrast with its irregular layout. The gardens were designed by Gertrude Jekyll. Marsh Court was a school from 1948 until 1989.

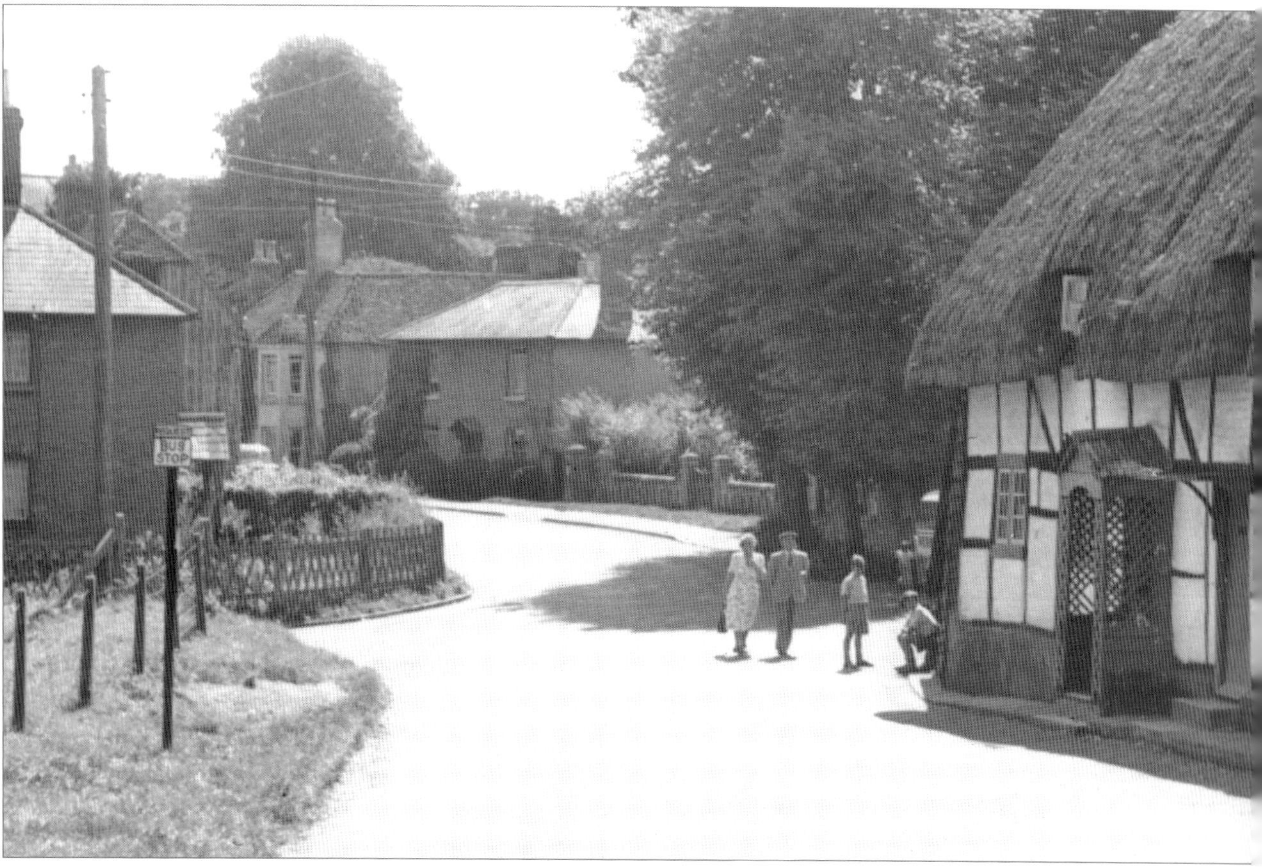

BROUGHTON, *Dog Lane c1955* B897011

This village is situated on the Wallop Brook, which flows south to join the Test at Bossington. Dog Lane now answers to the name of Queenswood Road, a clear indication of a rise in its fortunes. In the late 18th century the northern side of Dog Lane was 'waste', land too poor to interest landlords, and a number of squatters built hovels there. This mix of cottages represents the next generation, but while young children play happily in the sun, the gas lamp in the left foreground has seen better days. In the early 20th century Broughton's would-be Boy Scouts met in a cottage in Dog Lane, with just 'a hat and pole' as uniform.

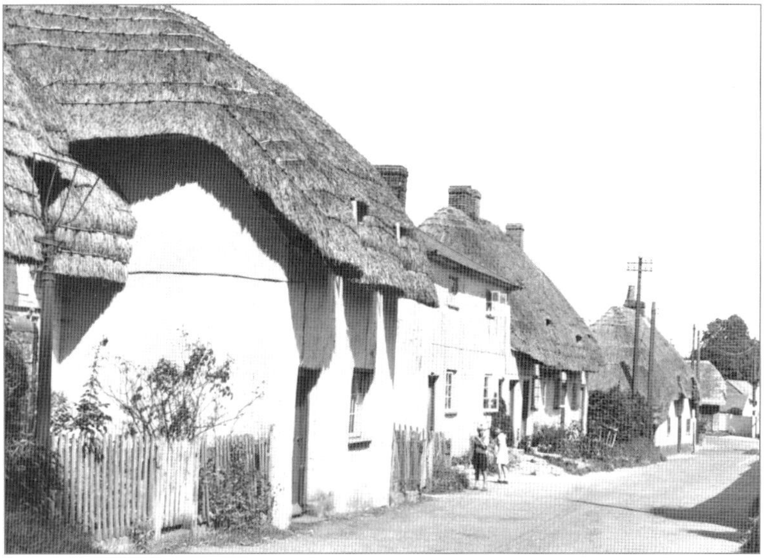

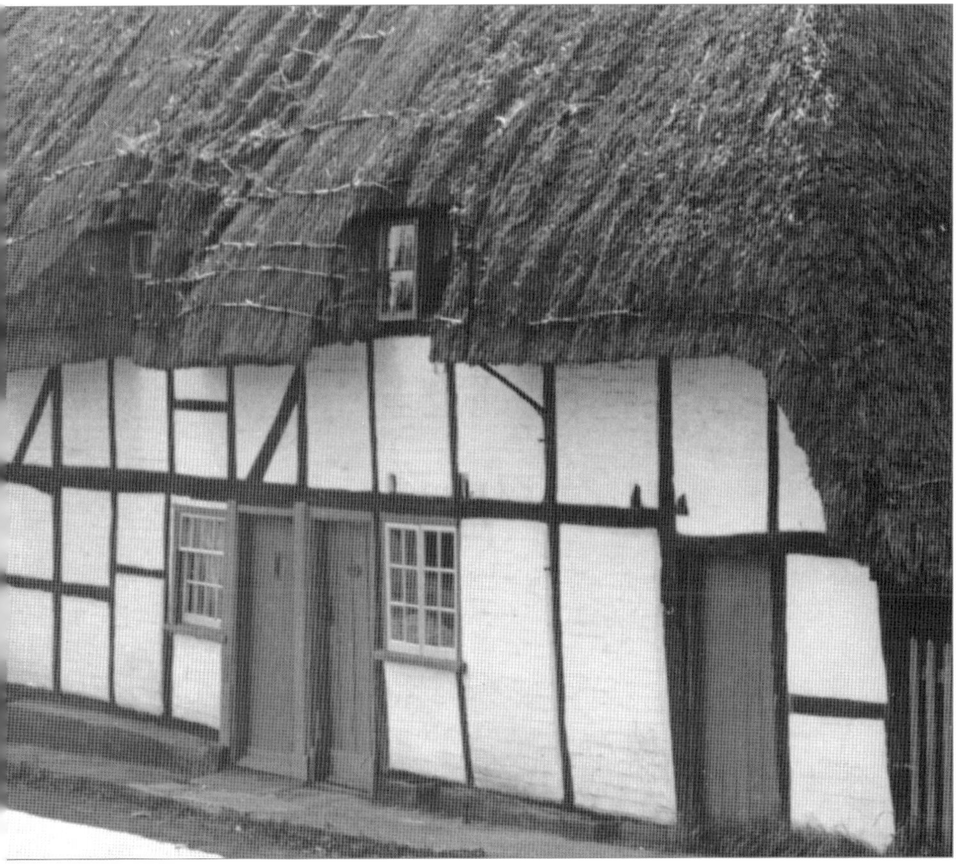

BROUGHTON *North End c1955* B897002

The enclosure awards of 1790 changed the pattern of landholdings in Broughton, and much of the farming was carried out from farmsteads or farm-places. These consisted of a dwelling with an attached yard enclosed by a high cob wall. North End probably began life as such a farmhouse with an associated barn or cottage and a yard, called a 'backside' or 'barton'.

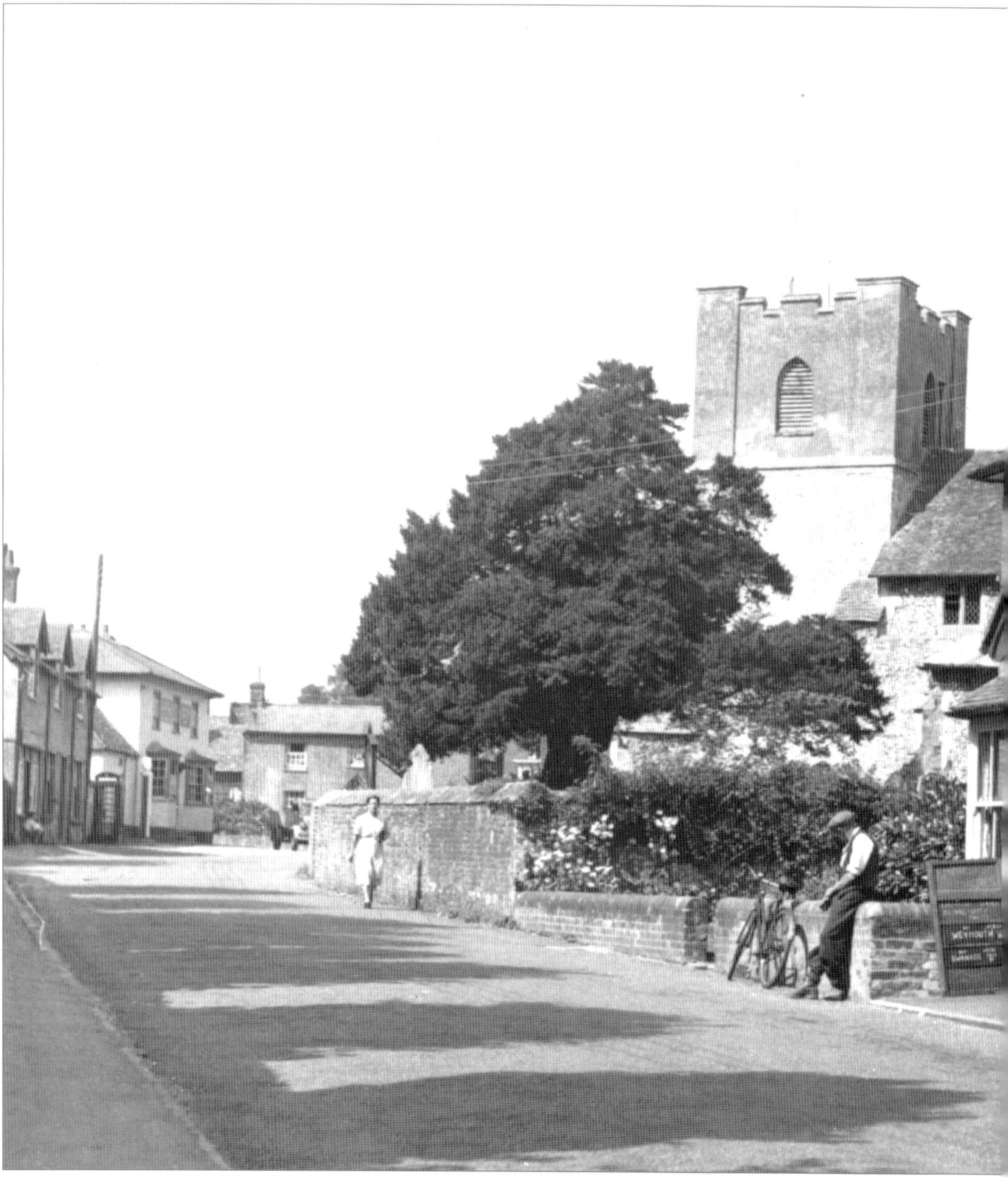

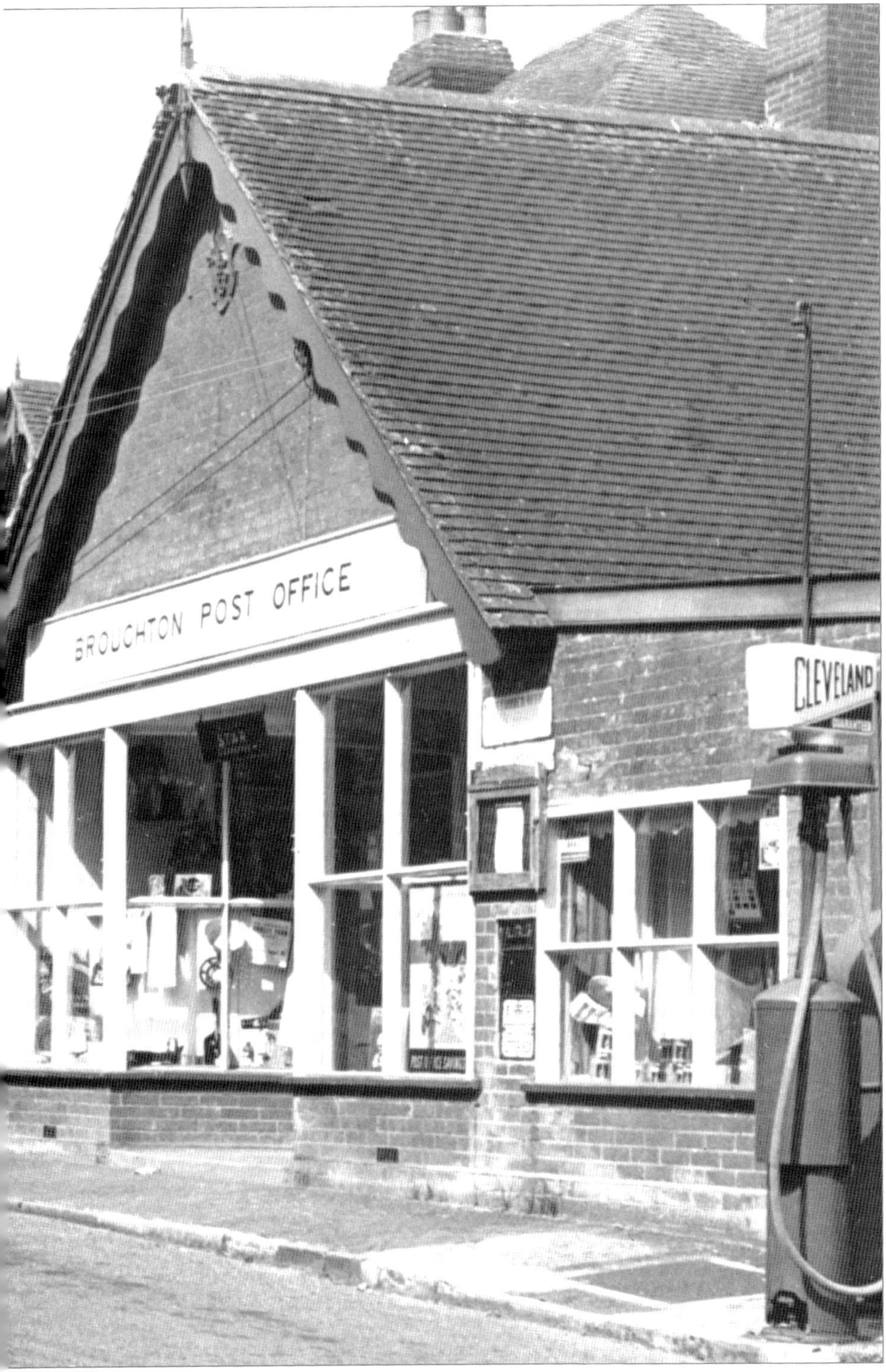

BROUGHTON
The Post Office and the Church c1955 B897009

St Mary's Church is of 12th- to 13th-century origin, and the interior is more interesting than the exterior, as this view tends to confirm. The post office dates to 1912; it was built by Charles Butt, who began as a cycle agent in Nether Wallop and arrived in Broughton in 1903. Five years later he bought a number of properties, including the smithy cottages for £155. These were demolished to make way for the post office, and the business remained here until 1980. On offer (on the board outside) in 1955 were 'Empress Coaches trips to Weymouth and Swanage', fuelled, no doubt, by Cleveland petrol (right), which flowed from the 1950s to 1972.

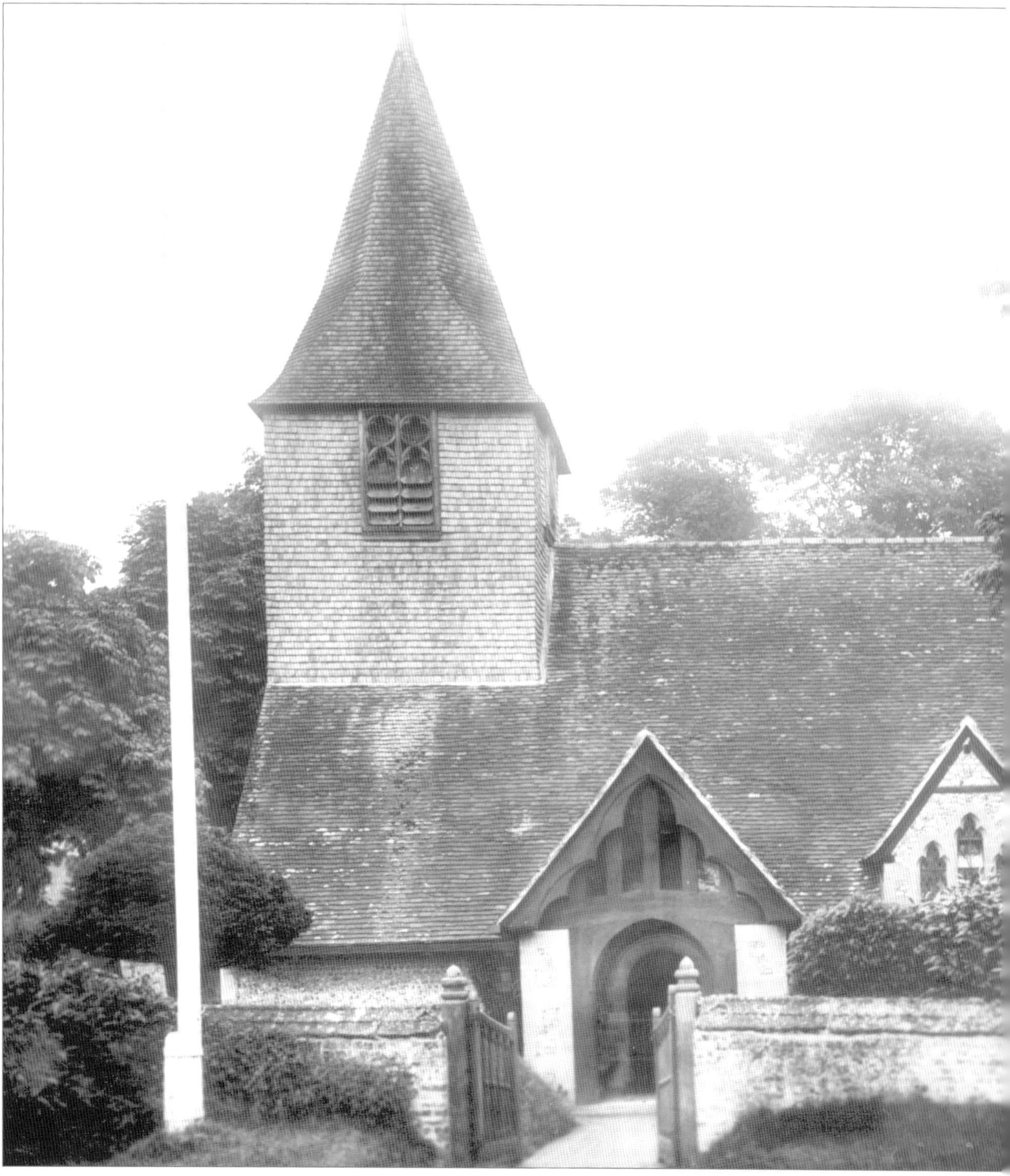

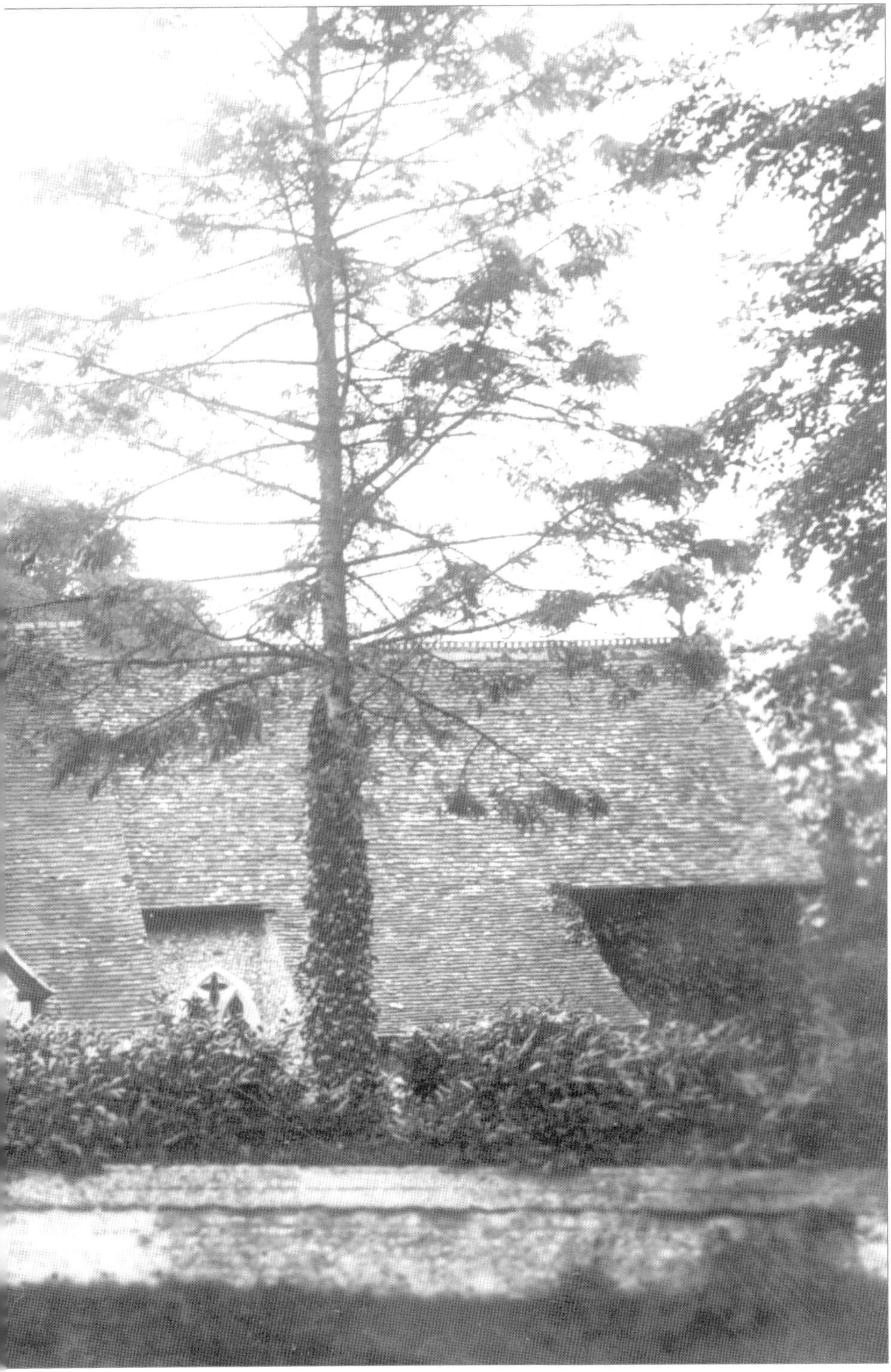

HOUGHTON
All Saints' Church
1904 51452

This low church is 12th- to 13th-century in the main, enlivened by a Victorian timber-framed and shingled bell turret carrying a small broach spire at its west end. The porch is also a Victorian addition. Inside, on some columns, are crosses carved by pilgrims on their way to visit St Swithun's shrine at Winchester.

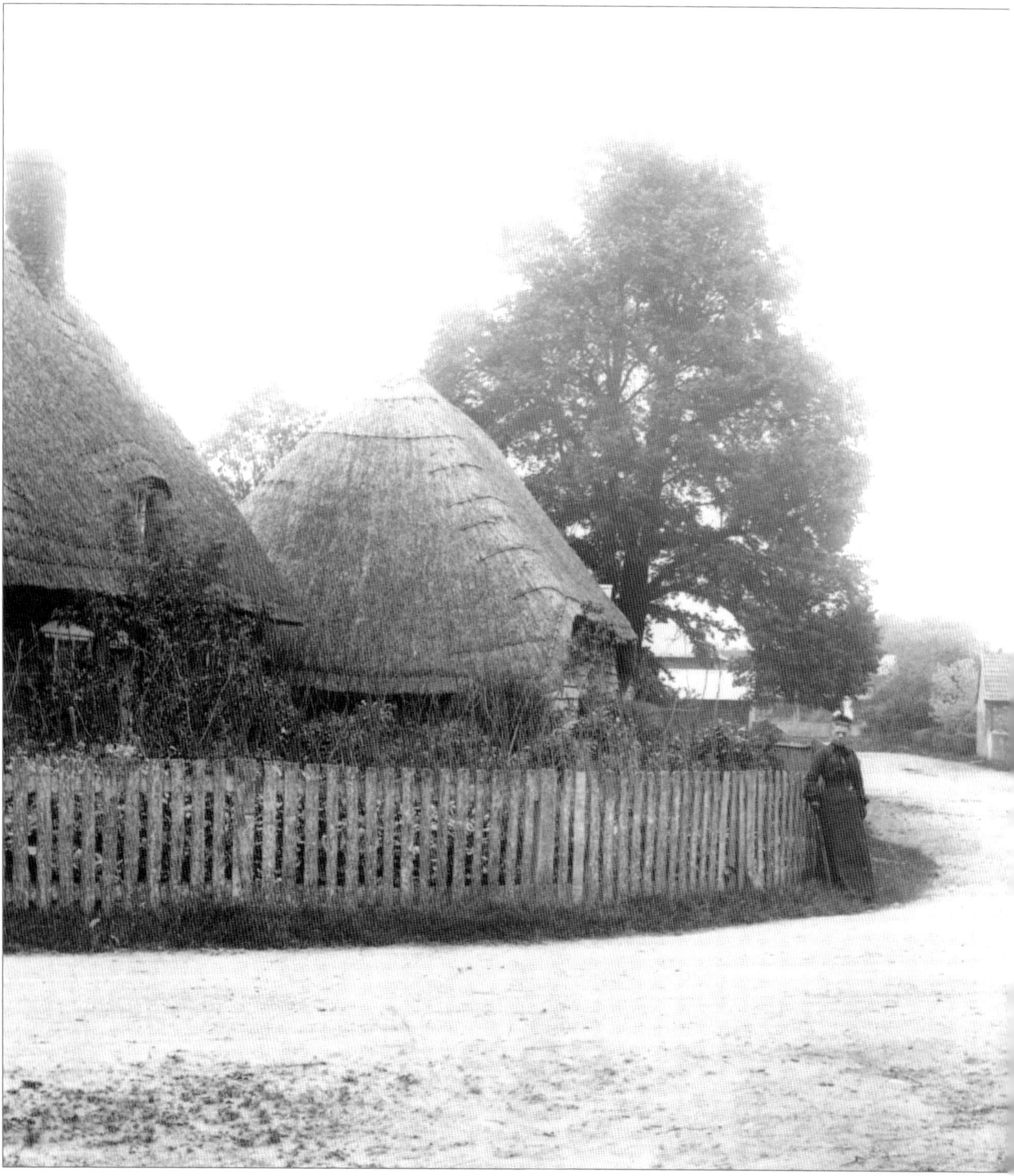

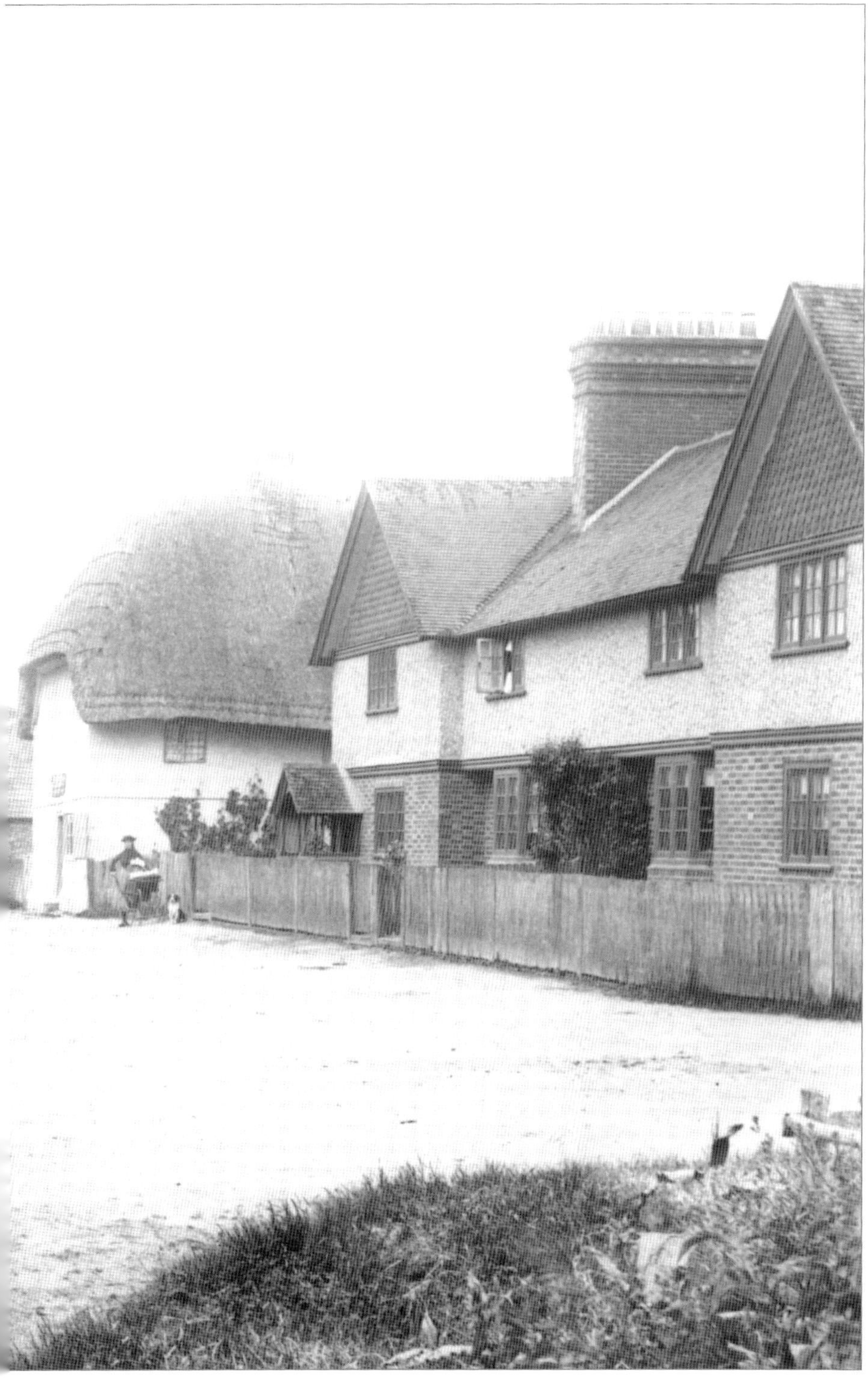

HOUGHTON
The Village 1904 51450

Houghton is a single street village running parallel with the Test, rather spread out, with numerous Edwardian estate cottages. Where the road through the village meets the road to Bossington stands Corner Cottage, far left, formerly the Old Dairy House, dating from the 18th century. On the corner itself an old lady strikes an austere pose. Across the street are some new estate cottages, in front of which a child takes a babe and a spaniel for a walk.

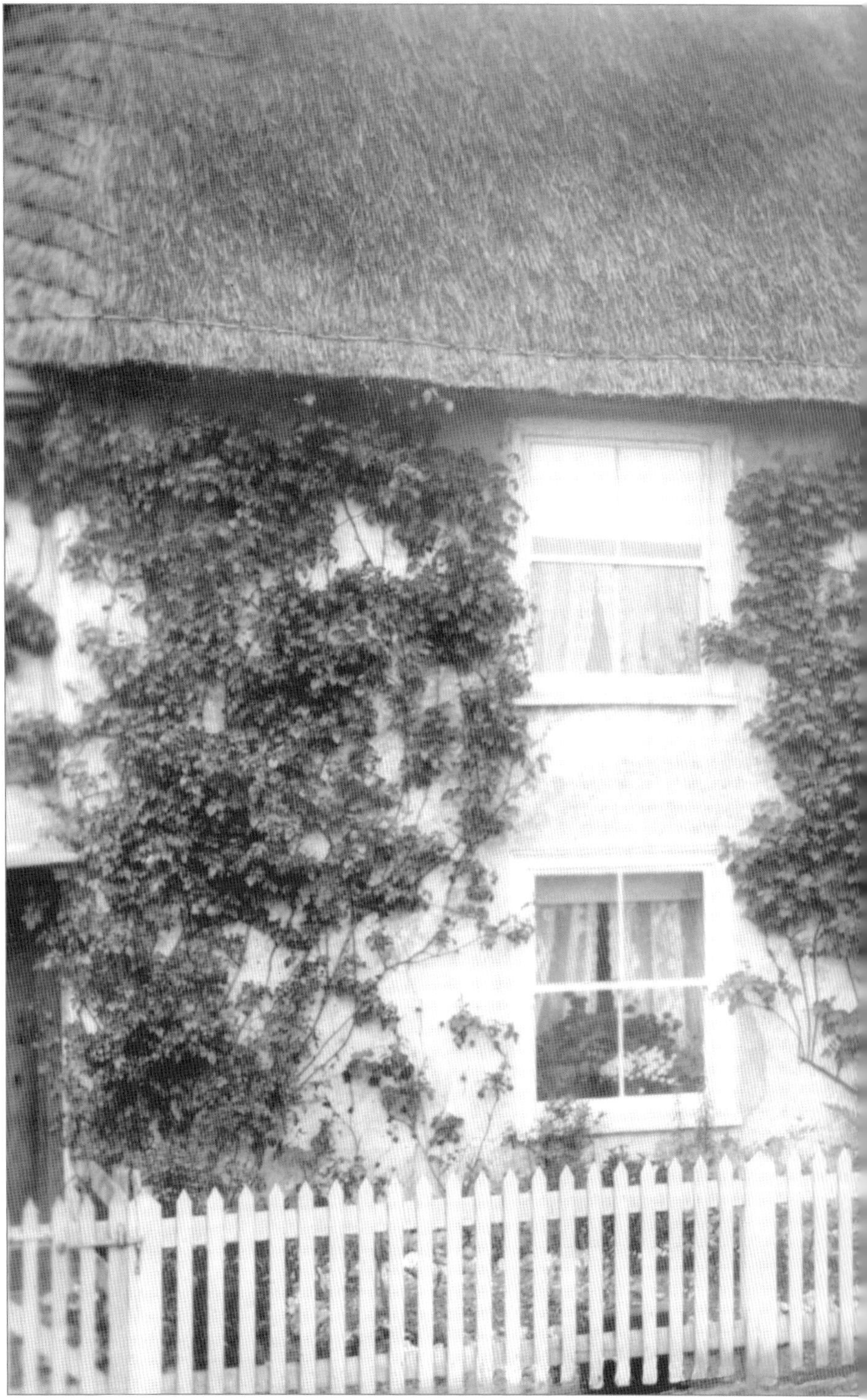

HOUGHTON
The Post Office 1904 51457

The first dedicated post office in England opened in 1845 at Kings Worthy, near Winchester, not far from the Test Valley. It is not known when Houghton Post Office first welcomed customers, but it looks well established in this early Edwardian view. Perhaps that is because the timber-framed and neatly thatched building that houses it is already over 300 years old. The telegraph office is well signed, and served by pole and wire. Telegrams were a well-used post office monopoly; the telephone did not arrive until the 1920s. The postman poses in uniform, mailbag at the ready over his shoulder. The sub-postmistress at this date was Miss Susannah Chandler.

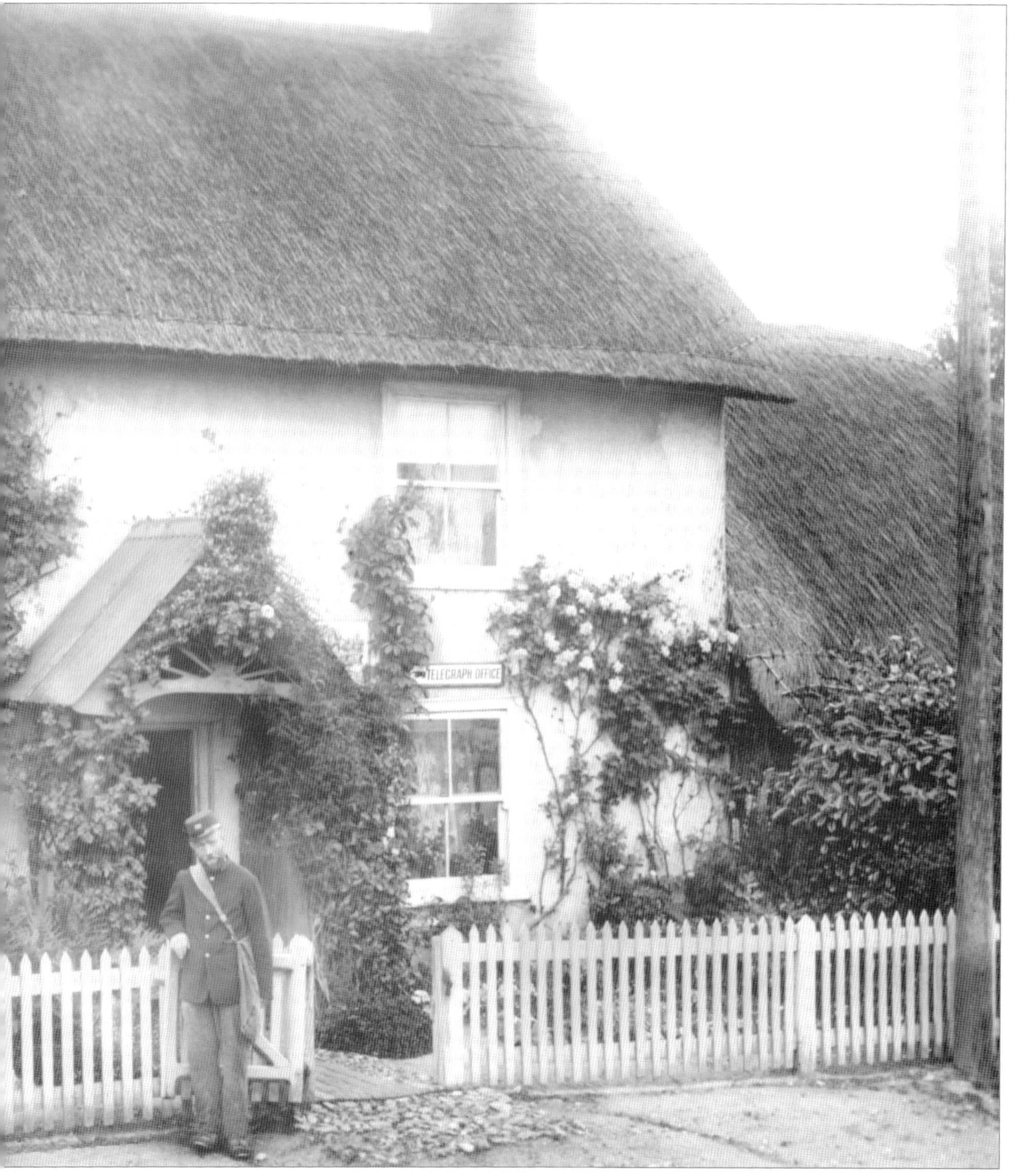
TELEGRAPH OFFICE

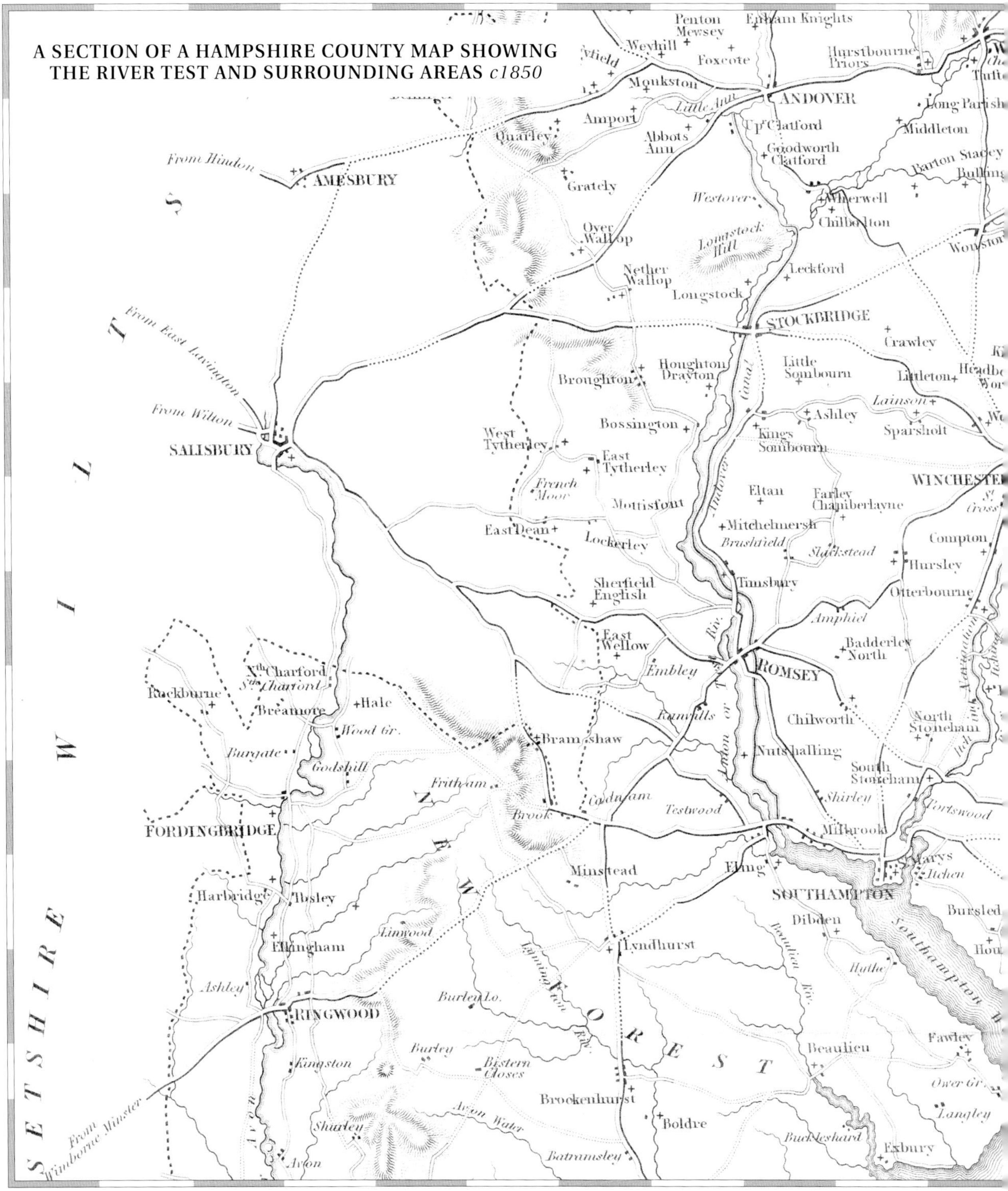

A SECTION OF A HAMPSHIRE COUNTY MAP SHOWING THE RIVER TEST AND SURROUNDING AREAS *c1850*

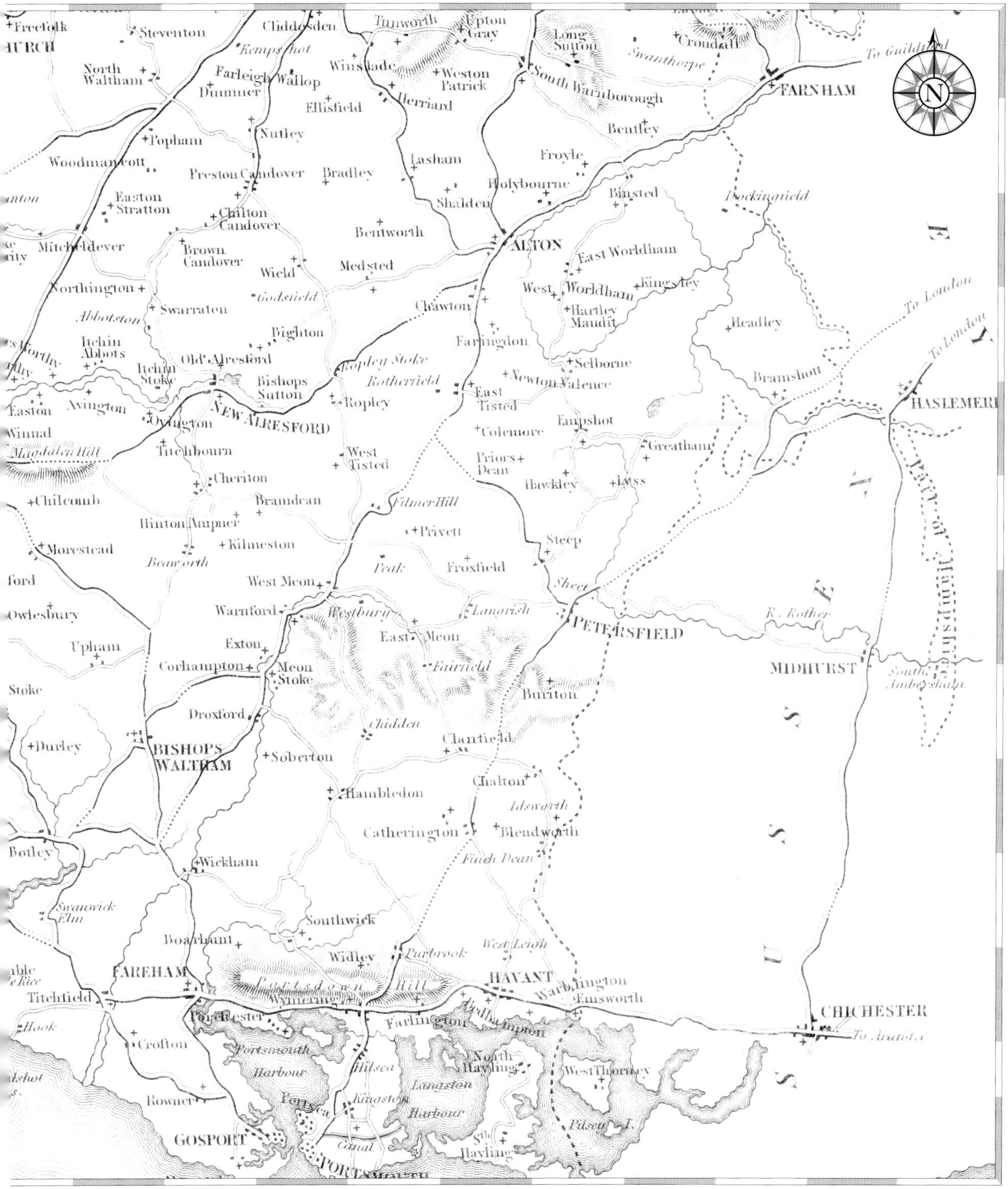
Freefolk
Steventon
Cliddesden
Tunworth
Upton Gray
Long Sutton
Croudall
To Guildford
North Waltham
Kempshot
Farleigh Wallop
Dummer
Winslade
Weston Patrick
South Warnborough
Swanthorpe
FARNHAM
Herriard
Ellisfield
Nutley
Bentley
Popham
Woodmancott
Preston Candover
Bradley
Lasham
Froyle
Holybourne
Shalden
Binsted
Dockingfield
Easton Stratton
Chilton Candover
Bentworth
Micheldever
Brown Candover
Wield
Medsted
ALTON
East Worldham
West Worldham
Kingsley
Godsfield
Northington
Abbotston
Swarraton
Chawton
Hartley Maudit
To London
Headley
Bighton
Itchin Abbots
Itchin Stoke
Old Alresford
Faringdon
Ropley Stoke
Rotherfield
Bishops Sutton
Newton Valence
Selborne
Bramshott
HASLEMERE
Easton
Avington
Ropley
East Tisted
Emshot
NEW ALRESFORD
Ovington
Colemore
Greatham
Winnal
Magdalen Hill
Titchbourn
West Tisted
Priors Dean
Hawkley
Lyss
Cheriton
Bramdean
Chilcomb
Filmer Hill
Hinton Ampner
Privett
Steep
Morestead
Kilmeston
Beaworth
Peak
Froxfield
West Meon
Sheet
Warnford
Westbury
Langrish
PETERSFIELD
R. Rother
Owlesbury
East Meon
Exton
Upham
Corhampton
Meon Stoke
Fairfield
MIDHURST
South Ambershain
Part of Hampshire
Stoke
Buriton
Droxford
Chidden
Clanfield
Durley
BISHOPS WALTHAM
Soberton
Chalton
Hambledon
Idsworth
Catherington
Blendworth
Botley
Wickham
Finch Dean
Swanwick Elm
Southwick
Boarhunt
West Leigh
Widley
Purbrook
FAREHAM
Portsdown Hill
Wymering
HAVANT
Warblington
Emsworth
Titchfield
Portchester
Farlington
Bedhampton
CHICHESTER
To Arundel
Hook
Crofton
Portsmouth Harbour
Hilsea
North Hayling
West Thorney
Langston Harbour
Rowner
Portsea
Kingston
Pilsey I.
GOSPORT
Canal
Sth Hayling
PORTSMOUTH
SUSSEX

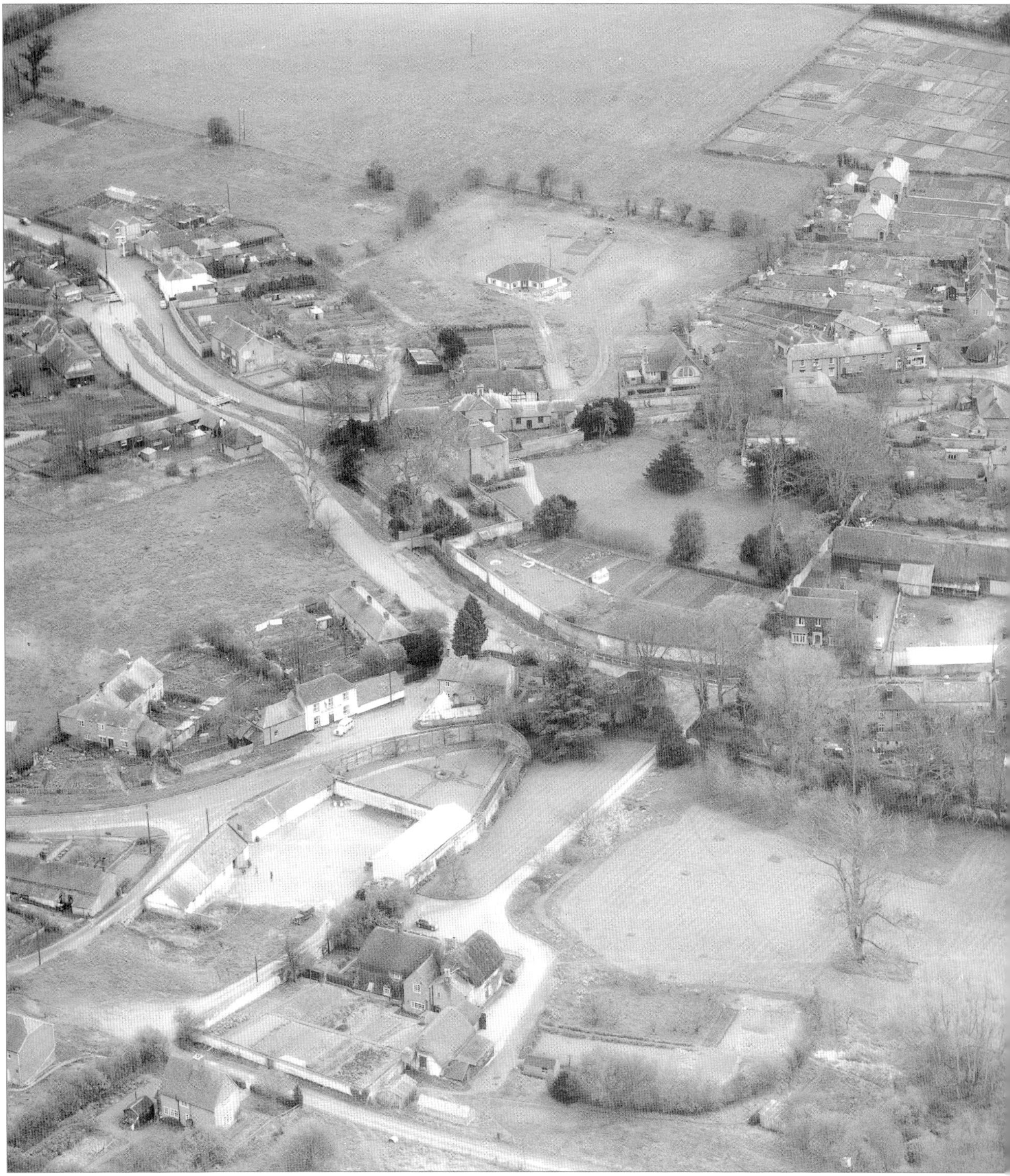

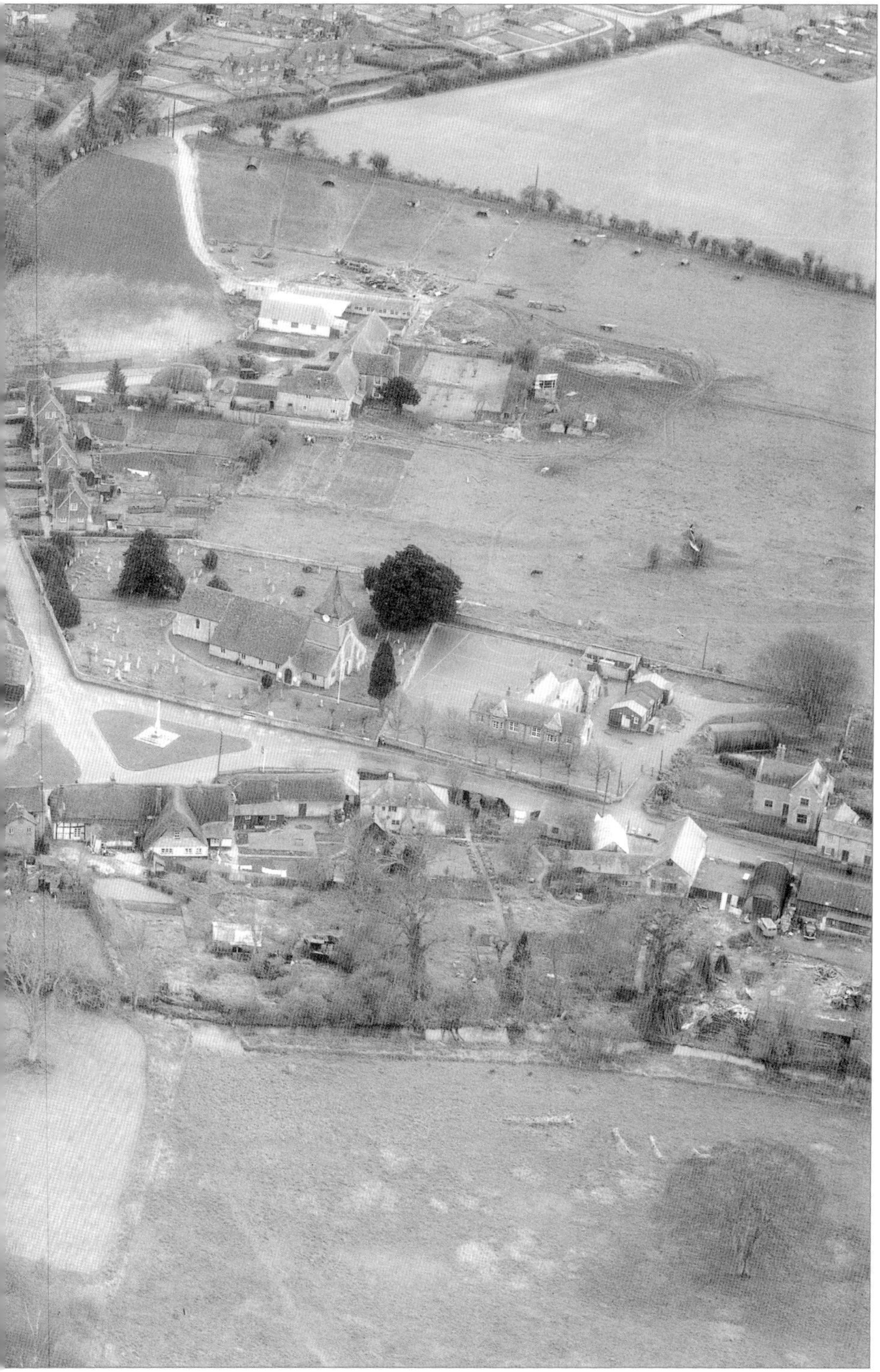

KINGS SOMBORNE
From the Air
1959 AFA74656

The village belonged to the king at Domesday, and to John of Gaunt in the 13th century. Earthwork traces of his 'palace' can be seen above and to the right of the church of St Peter and St Paul. More readily visible is the war memorial, designed by Lutyens, thanks to the generosity of Herbert Johnson of Marsh Court. This large village has many thatched buildings, particularly along the road to Little Somborne, where there is a cruck cottage.

KINGS SOMBORNE
The Village
c1955 K99002

The two-storey brick dwelling with hipped slate roof in the centre of this view is Pear Tree Cottage. In the foreground is a group of timber-framed cottages, originally three, with colour-washed brick infilling and neatly thatched roof. The cottage has fared better than the picket fence. The dog has spotted something of interest on the road from the south.

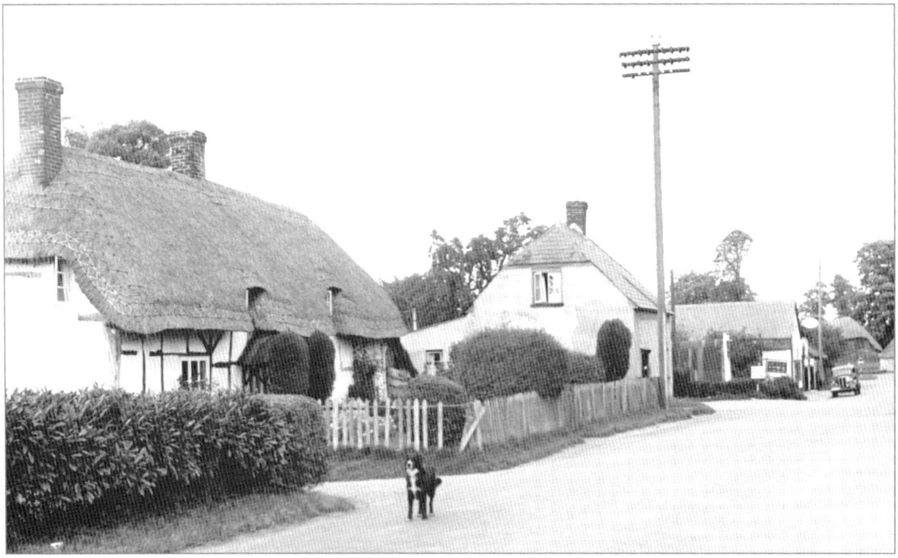

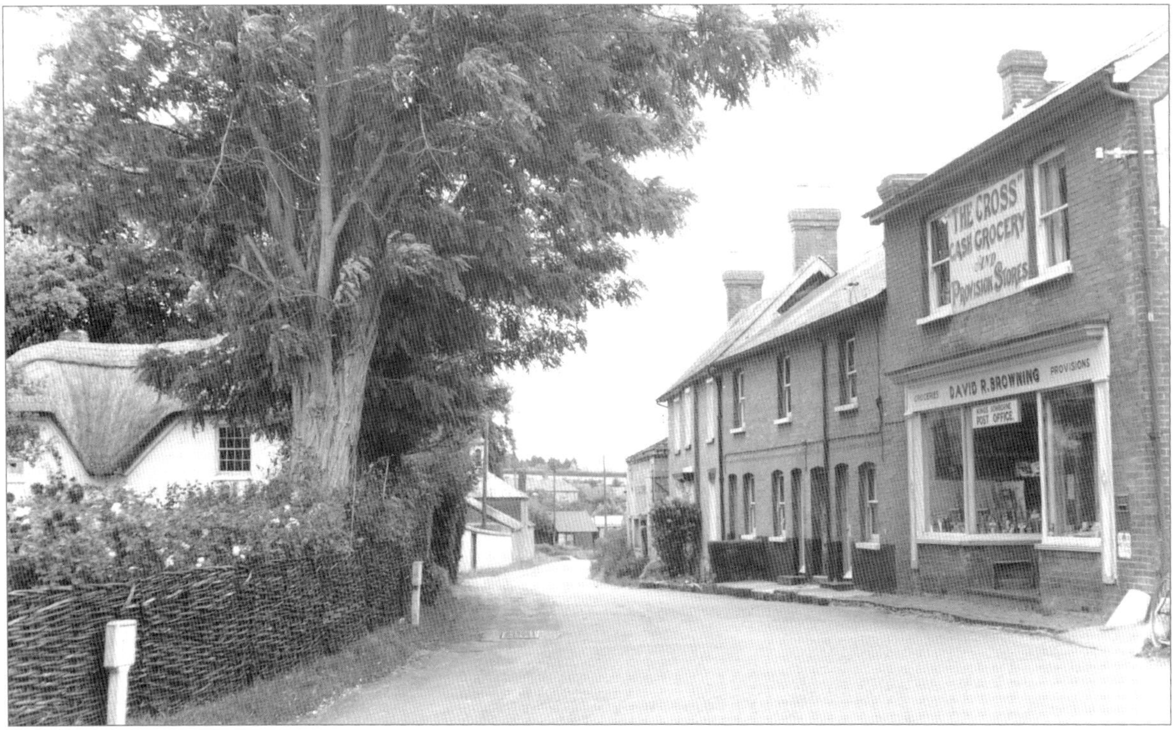

KINGS SOMBORNE, *The Post Office c1955* K99013

This Victorian and Edwardian terrace has long housed the village post office, and at this date The Cross Cash Grocery and Provision Stores was in the care of David R Browning. Kings Somborne once had a wide array of stores, including at one stage a fish and chip shop, but it saw five businesses close their doors in the 1970s and 80s.

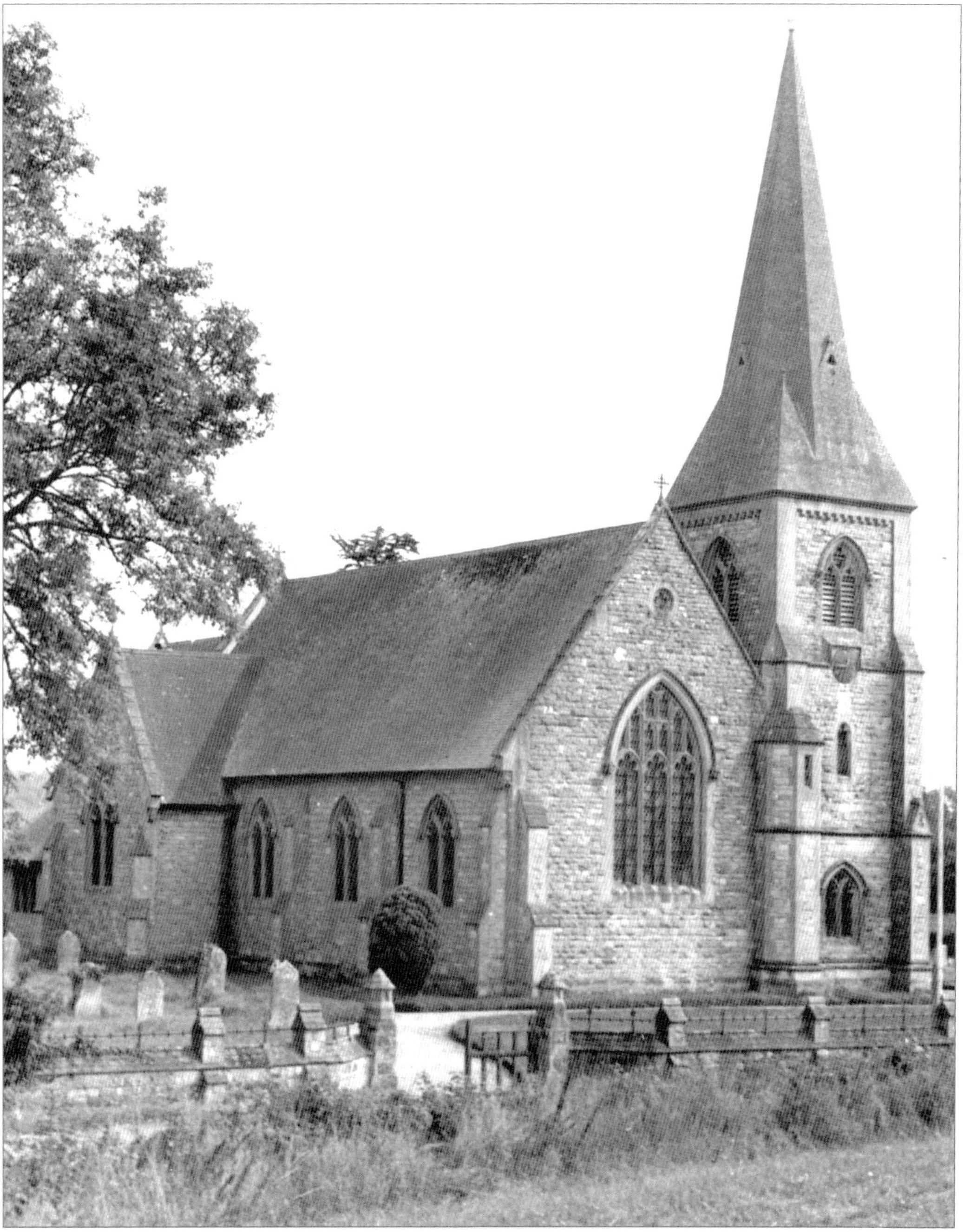

LOCKERLEY, *St John the Evangelist's Church c1955* L367025

This church was built in 1888-90 at the behest of Frederick Dalgety, squire of Lockerley, at a cost of £7,000; the architect was J Colson. The south-west tower carries a stone broach spire, and a small Norman window from the earlier church is also woven into the fabric. The ground plan of the Norman church is marked out alongside.

▼ **LOCKERLEY,** *The Green c1955* L367016

Lockerley is a very scattered settlement, characterised by its expansive greens, and it stands in an area of clayey soil. Lockerley boasts four greens, including Butts Green where archery practice no doubt took place. This is plain Lockerley Green; the post office is the white-fronted building beside the car and phone box. In the distance is the Baptist Providence Chapel. Mr Alfred Pegler of Southampton laid the foundation stone here on 23 February 1880.

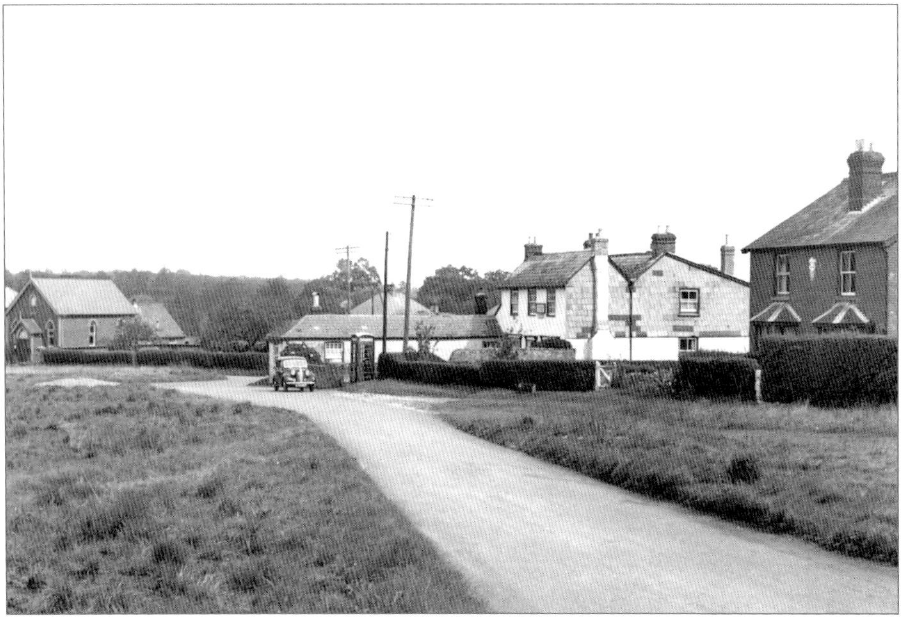

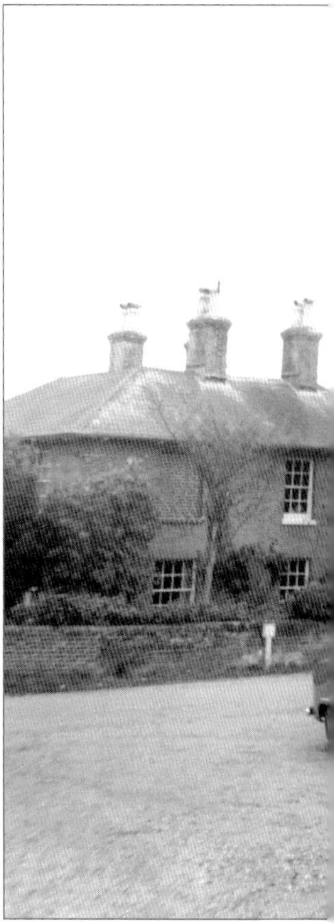

► **SHERFIELD ENGLISH**
St Leonard's Church c1965 S630018

This is the third church to serve the village; it was built in 1903 by Fred Bath of Salisbury at the expense of Lady Ashburton, who wished to commemorate her only daughter. It is in red brick and stone. The crossing tower, with octagonal bell-stage, is connected by flying buttresses to four big pinnacles, and there is a spire as well. Lavish is too small a word.

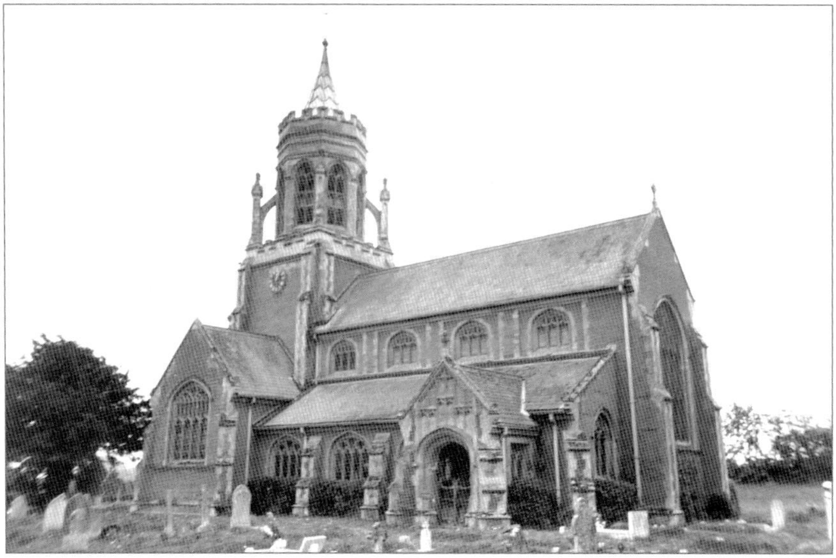

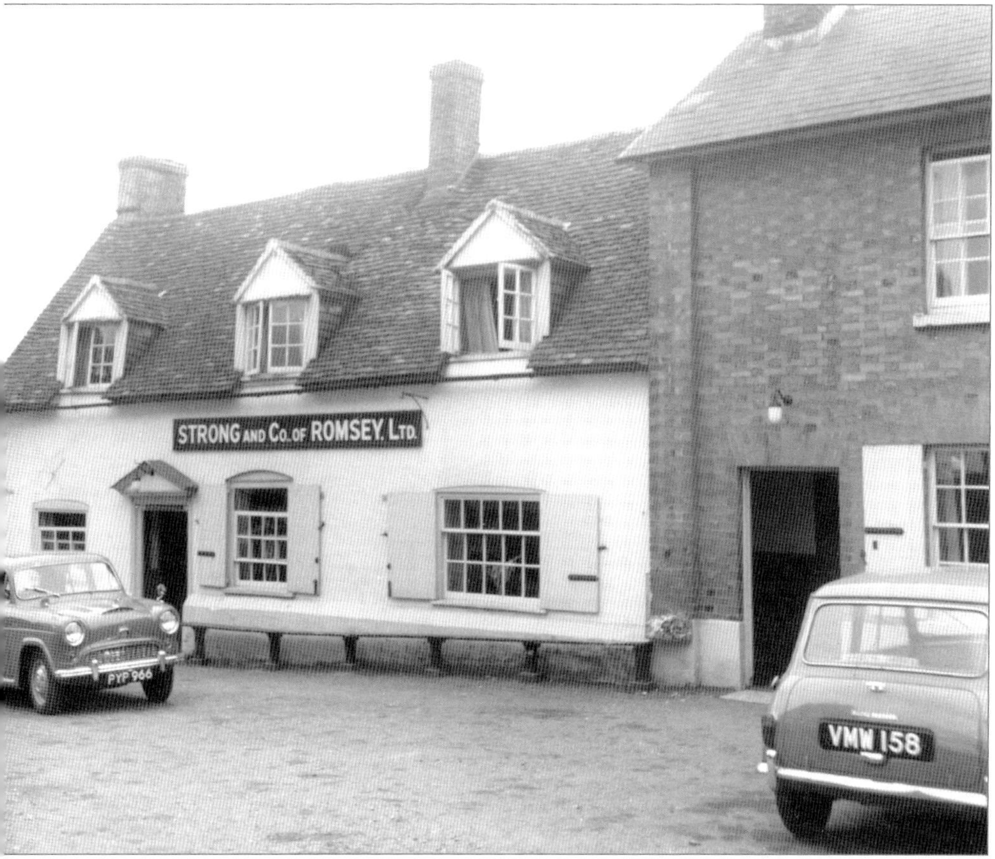

◄ **SHERFIELD ENGLISH**
The Hatchet Inn c1965 S630008

There is little obvious custom for the 18th-century Hatchet Inn, and no signage other than Strong & Co of Romsey Ltd. David Faber, of the publishing family, bought up three ailing breweries in the town and united them under the name of the biggest. It made for some memorable marketing – posters with the slogan 'You are in the Strong Country', for example.

► **ROMSEY,** *The Abbey 1899* 42975

Romsey grew as a bridging point on the Test for roads to Salisbury, Winchester and Stockbridge. The impressive abbey dominates the scene. The Abbey Church of St Mary and St Ethelfleda is one of the finest examples of Norman architecture in Europe. It stands on the site of a nunnery founded by Edward the Elder in AD907. The present church dates from 1120. At the Dissolution (1539) the townspeople, who had been using it as a parish church, were able to purchase it for £100.

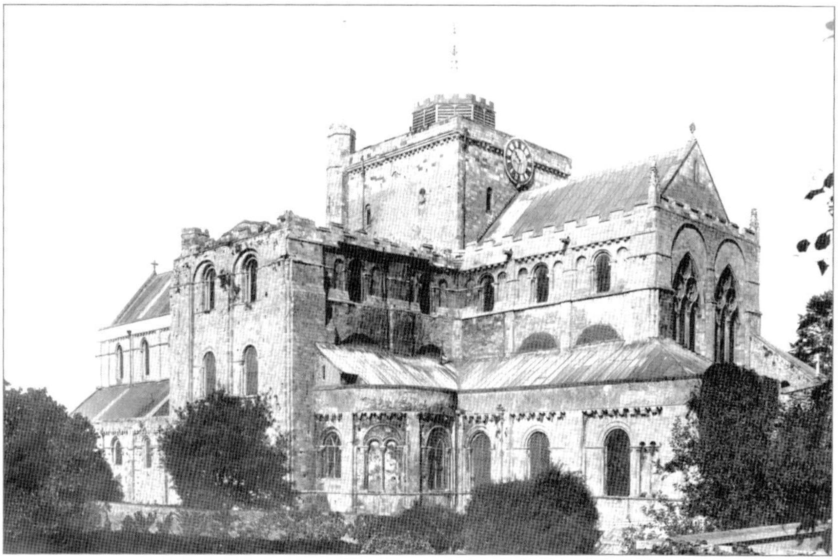

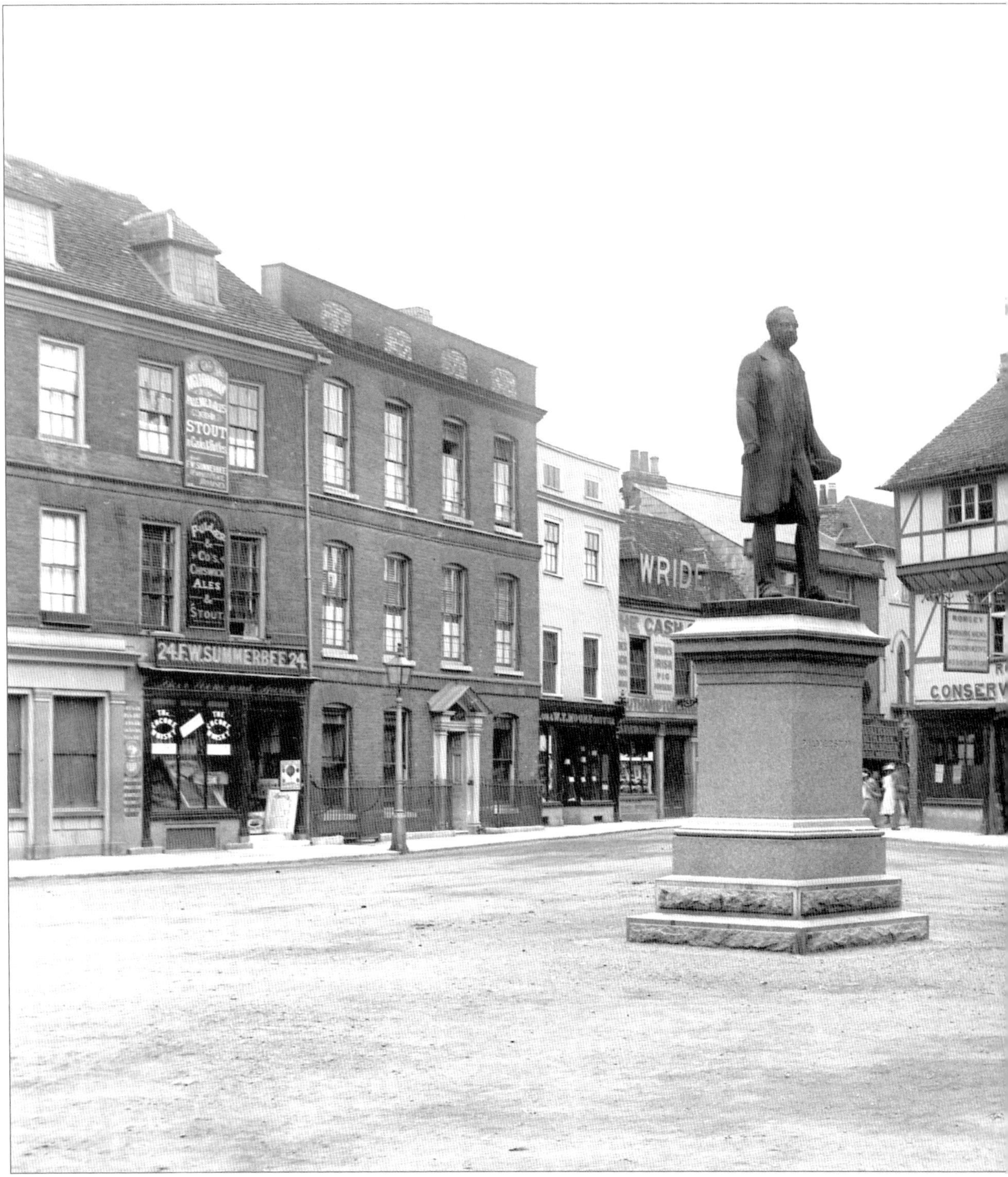
STOUT
ALES
&
STOUT
24 F.W. SUMMERBEE 24
WRIDE
CONSERV

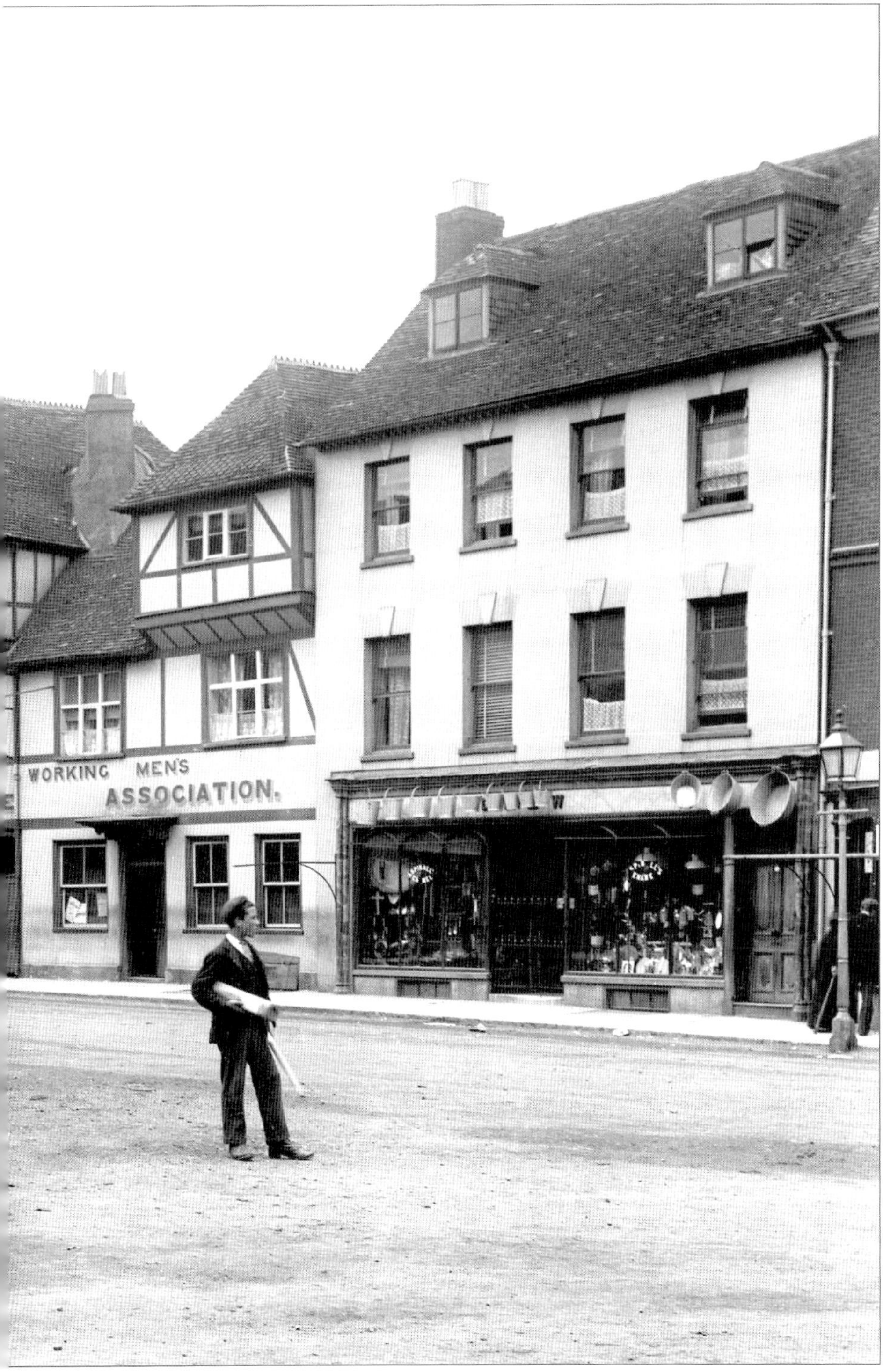

ROMSEY
The Palmerston Monument 1898 42103

The bronze statue of Lord Palmerston by Matthew Noble was erected in 1867. It gazes impassively out across the Market Place, strangely mimicked by the only inhabitant in close view. Behind his lordship, F W Summerbee's shop is selling The Encore Whisky and Fuller & Co's Chiswick Ales & Stouts, while Wride's a few doors down specialise in 'Irish Pig Powders'. The Conservative Association's building (centre right), until four years previously the Swan Inn, had seen many episodes of Romsey's history enacted, including the execution by hanging from its own elaborate bracket of two Civil War soldiers. Next door, H Drew, cutler, gun maker, and ironmonger, 'respectfully invited the attention of Housekeepers to his recent consignment of Ironmongery Goods'.

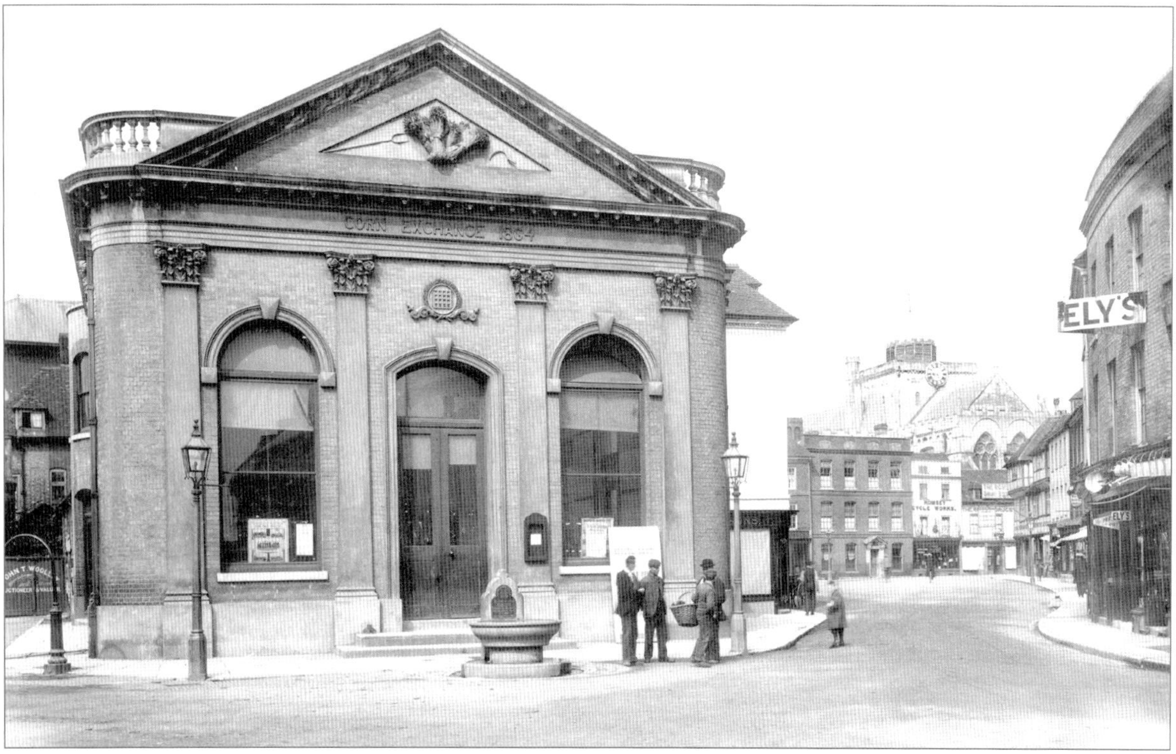

▲ **ROMSEY,** *The Corn Exchange 1903* 49338

This is a wonderful building, surprisingly classical for its date of construction - 1864. Its three bays are divided by giant Corinthian pilasters, and the pediment contains a relief of sheaves, a sickle and a pitchfork. Posters ask for volunteers for the militia – the building served as their headquarters. In the street stand a marble fountain, presented to the town by Lord Mount-Temple in 1886, and a group of fellows, presumably not discussing militia matters. To the right is Thomas Ely & Sons, ironmongers, who 20 years later entertained the town by broadcasting radio concerts from their upstairs window. To the left are the ornate gates of John T Woolley, livestock auctioneer - sheep sales a speciality, no doubt.

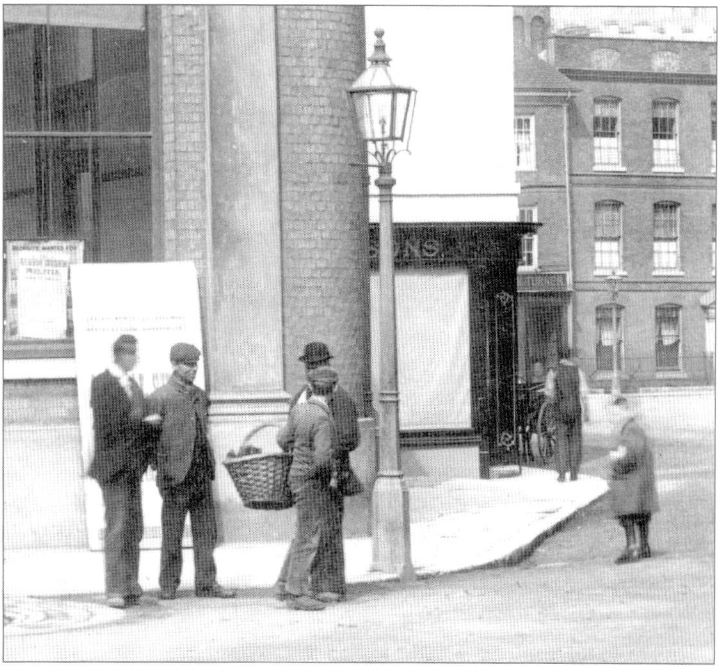

► *detail from* 49338

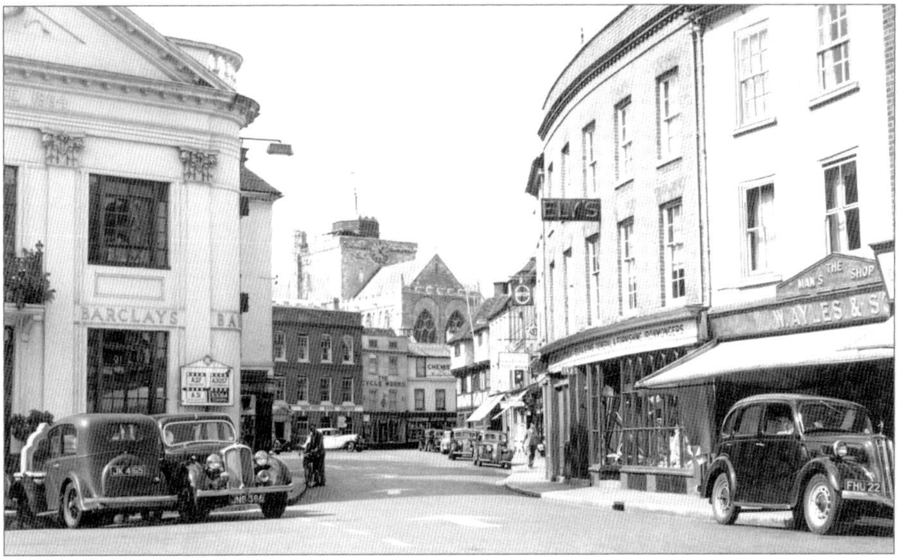

ROMSEY
The Market Place c1955 R53019

Half a century after 49338 (opposite) was taken, there is a new role for the Corn Exchange as a branch of Barclays Bank. In the distance the largest of the three premises houses the Midland Bank; next to it is the Cycle Works, and next to that a chemist's shop. Now it is cars that are more likely to congregate outside the Corn Exchange than people, and road signs have begun to appear.

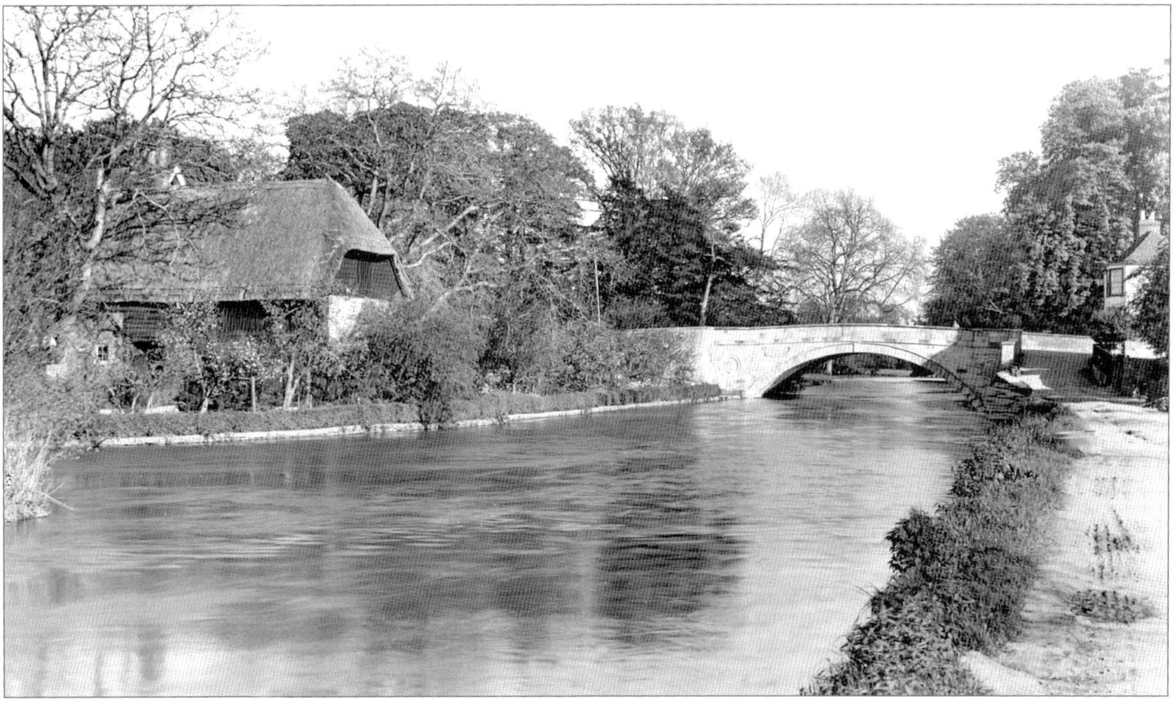

ROMSEY, *Middlebridge and the River Test 1932* 85042

The potential force of river currents is evident even in a peaceful view such as this; by the late 18th century they had seriously weakened the three-arch medieval bridge carrying the main route from Romsey to the west. Lord Palmerston agreed that the river could be diverted, and in 1783 Robert Mylne replaced the tottering structure with 'one beautiful segmental arch'. It was rebuilt in1931.

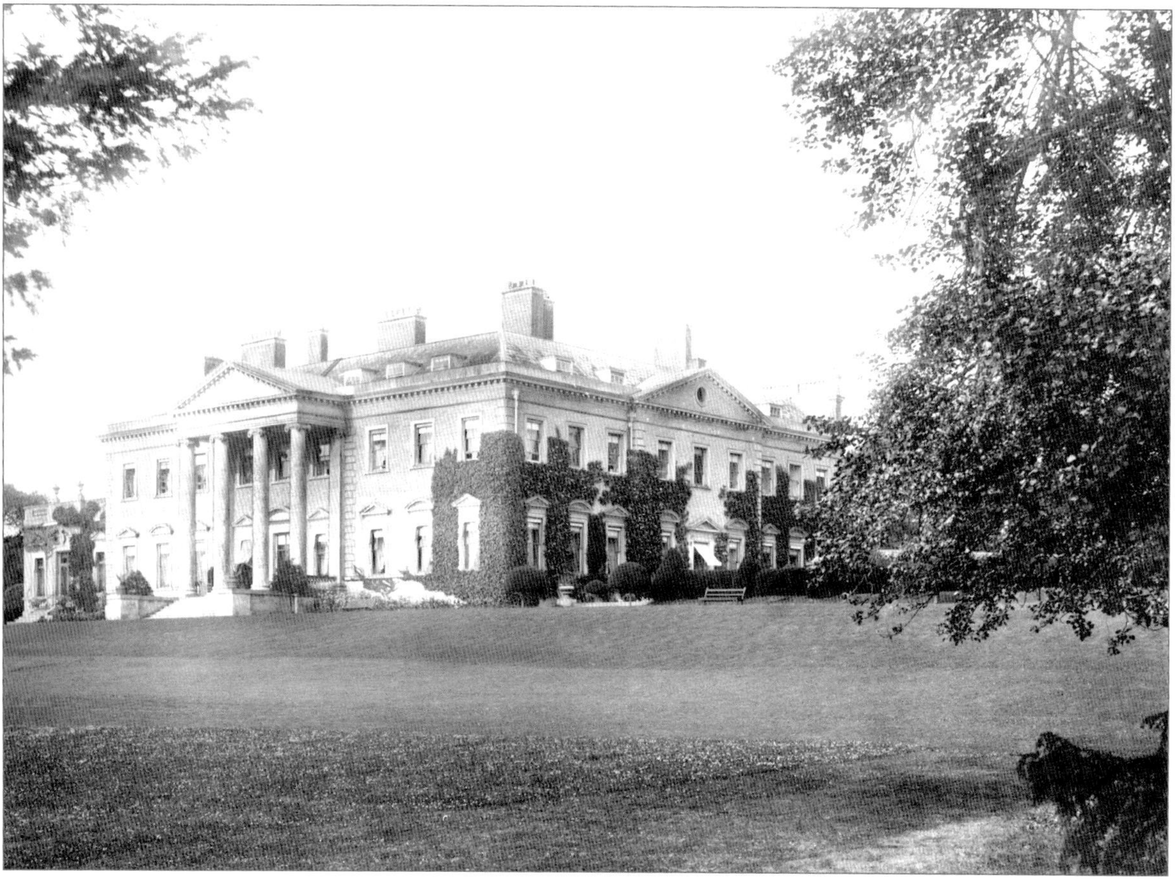

ROMSEY, *Broadlands 1904* 51447

The first building here probably dated from the early 16th century, and was associated with the management of fishponds. Major work by Sir Francis Fleming took place fifty years later, and the St Barbe family continued to develop the site, particularly the gardens. In 1736 the 1st Lord Palmerston bought the estate for £26,000, and his grandson, the 2nd Lord Palmerston, was largely responsible for the later appearance of Broadlands. He employed Lancelot 'Capability' Brown from 1767 to 1779 to create a Palladian mansion in a landscaped park. In a second phase of work, Brown's son-in-law, Henry Holland, remodelled the east front and built the Ionic portico.

INDEX

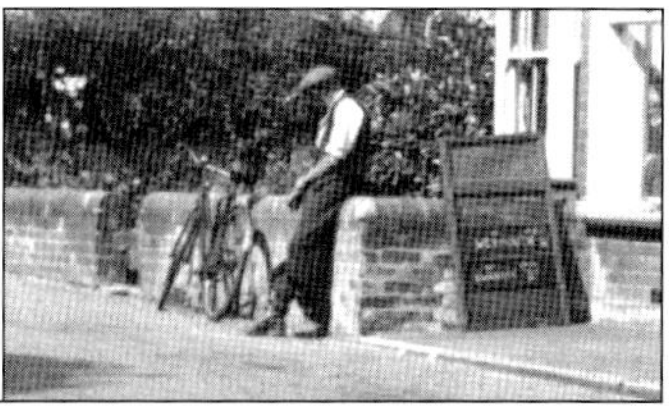

The Francis Frith Collection Titles

www.francisfrith.com

The Francis Frith Collection publishes over 100 new titles each year. A selection of those currently available is listed below. For latest catalogue please contact The Francis Frith Collection.
Town Books 96 pages, approximately 75 photos. ***County and Themed Books*** 128 pages, approximately 135 photos (unless specified). Pocket Albums are miniature editions of Frith local history books 128 pages, approximately 95 photos.

Accrington Old and New
Alderley Edge and Wilmslow
Amersham, Chesham and Rickmansworth
Andover
Around Abergavenny
Around Alton
Aylesbury
Barnstaple
Bedford
Bedfordshire
Berkshire Living Memories
Berkshire Pocket Album
Blackpool Pocket Album
Bognor Regis
Bournemouth
Bradford
Bridgend
Bridport
Brighton and Hove
Bristol
Buckinghamshire
Calne Living Memories
Camberley Pocket Album
Canterbury Cathedral
Cardiff Old and New
Chatham and the Medway Towns
Chelmsford
Chepstow Then and Now
Cheshire
Cheshire Living Memories
Chester
Chesterfield
Chigwell
Christchurch
Churches of East Cornwall
Clevedon
Clitheroe
Corby Living Memories
Cornish Coast
Cornwall Living Memories
Cotswold Living Memories
Cotswold Pocket Album
Coulsdon, Chipstead and Woodmanstern
County Durham
Cromer, Sheringham and Holt
Dartmoor Pocket Album
Derby
Derbyshire
Derbyshire Living Memories
Devon
Devon Churches
Dorchester
Dorset Coast Pocket Album
Dorset Living Memories
Dorset Villages
Down the Dart
Down the Severn
Down the Thames
Dunmow, Thaxted and Finchingfield
Durham
East Anglia Pocket Album
East Devon
East Grinstead
Edinburgh
Ely and The Fens
Essex Pocket Album
Essex Second Selection
Essex: The London Boroughs
Exeter
Exmoor
Falmouth
Farnborough, Fleet and Aldershot
Folkestone
Frome
Furness and Cartmel Peninsulas
Glamorgan
Glasgow
Glastonbury
Gloucester
Gloucestershire
Greater Manchester
Guildford
Hailsham
Hampshire
Harrogate
Hastings and Bexhill
Haywards Heath Living Memories
Heads of the Valleys
Heart of Lancashire Pocket Album
Helston
Herefordshire
Horsham
Humberside Pocket Album
Huntingdon, St Neots and St Ives
Hythe, Romney Marsh and Ashford
Ilfracombe
Ipswich Pocket Album
Isle of Wight
Isle of Wight Living Memories
King's Lynn
Kingston upon Thames
Lake District Pocket Album
Lancashire Living Memories
Lancashire Villages

Available from your local bookshop or from the publisher

Lancaster, Morecambe and Heysham Pocket Album
Leeds Pocket Album
Leicester
Leicestershire
Lincolnshire Living Memoires
Lincolnshire Pocket Album
Liverpool and Merseyside
London Pocket Album
Ludlow
Maidenhead
Maidstone
Malmesbury
Manchester Pocket Album
Marlborough
Matlock
Merseyside Living Memories
Nantwich and Crewe
New Forest
Newbury Living Memories
Newquay to St Ives
North Devon Living Memories
North London
North Wales
North Yorkshire
Northamptonshire
Northumberland
Northwich
Nottingham
Nottinghamshire Pocket Album
Oakham
Odiham Then and Now
Oxford Pocket Album
Oxfordshire
Padstow
Pembrokeshire
Penzance
Petersfield Then and Now
Plymouth
Poole and Sandbanks
Preston Pocket Album
Ramsgate Old and New
Reading Pocket Album
Redditch Living Memories
Redhill to Reigate
Richmond
Ringwood
Rochdale
Romford Pocket Album
Salisbury Pocket Album
Scotland
Scottish Castles
Sevenoaks and Tonbridge
Sheffield and South Yorkshire Pocket Album
Shropshire
Somerset
South Devon Coast
South Devon Living Memories
South East London
Southampton Pocket Album
Southend Pocket Album
Southport
Southwold to Aldeburgh
Stourbridge Living Memories
Stratford upon Avon
Stroud
Suffolk
Suffolk Pocket Album
Surrey Living Memories
Sussex
Sutton
Swanage and Purbeck
Swansea Pocket Album
Swindon Living Memories
Taunton
Teignmouth
Tenby and Saundersfoot
Tiverton
Torbay
Truro
Uppingham
Villages of Kent
Villages of Surrey
Villages of Sussex Pocket Album
Wakefield and the Five Towns Living Memories
Warrington
Warwick
Warwickshire Pocket Album
Wellingborough Living Memories
Wells
Welsh Castles
West Midlands Pocket Album
West Wiltshire Towns
West Yorkshire
Weston-super-Mare
Weymouth
Widnes and Runcorn
Wiltshire Churches
Wiltshire Living Memories
Wiltshire Pocket Album
Wimborne
Winchester Pocket Album
Windermere
Windsor
Wirral
Wokingham and Bracknell
Woodbridge
Worcester
Worcestershire
Worcestershire Living Memories
Wyre Forest
York Pocket Album
Yorkshire
Yorkshire Coastal Memories
Yorkshire Dales
Yorkshire Revisited

See Frith books on the internet at www.francisfrith.com

FRITH PRODUCTS & SERVICES

Francis Frith would doubtless be pleased to know that the pioneering publishing venture he started in 1860 still continues today. Over a hundred and forty years later, The Francis Frith Collection continues in the same innovative tradition and is now one of the foremost publishers of vintage photographs in the world. Some of the current activities include:

INTERIOR DECORATION

Today Frith's photographs can be seen framed and as giant wall murals in thousands of pubs, restaurants, hotels, banks, retail stores and other public buildings throughout the country. In every case they enhance the unique local atmosphere of the places they depict and provide reminders of gentler days in an increasingly busy and frenetic world.

PRODUCT PROMOTIONS

Frith products are used by many major companies to promote the sales of their own products or to reinforce their own history and heritage. Frith promotions have been used by Hovis bread, Courage beers, Scots Porage Oats, Colman's mustard, Cadbury's foods, Mellow Birds coffee, Dunhill pipe tobacco, Guinness, and Bulmer's Cider.

GENEALOGY AND FAMILY HISTORY

As the interest in family history and roots grows world-wide, more and more people are turning to Frith's photographs of Great Britain for images of the towns, villages and streets where their ancestors lived; and, of course, photographs of the churches and chapels where their ancestors were christened, married and buried are an essential part of every genealogy tree and family album.

FRITH PRODUCTS

All Frith photographs are available Framed or just as Mounted Prints and Posters (size 23 x 16 inches). These may be ordered from the address below. Other products available are- Address Books, Calendars, Jigsaws, Canvas Prints, Notelets and local and prestige books.

THE INTERNET

Already ninety thousand Frith photographs can be viewed and purchased on the internet through the Frith websites and a myriad of partner sites.

For more detailed information on Frith companies and products, look at this site:
www.francisfrith.com

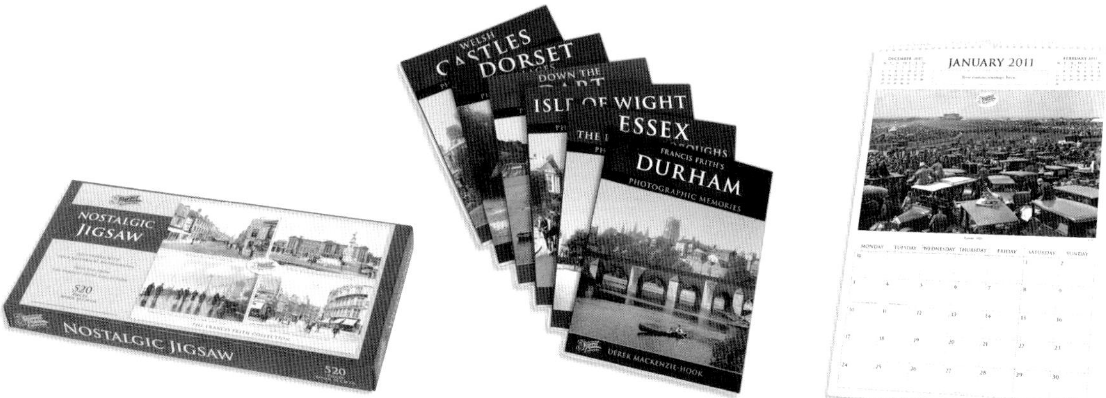

See the complete list of Frith Books at: www.francisfrith.com
This web site is regularly updated with the latest list of publications from The Francis Frith Collection. If you wish to buy books relating to another part of the country that your local bookshop does not stock, you may purchase on-line.

For further information, trade, or author enquiries please contact us at the address below:
The Francis Frith Collection, Unit 6, Oakley Business Park, Wylye Road, Dinton, Wiltshire SP3 5EU.
Tel: +44 (0)1722 716 376 Fax: +44 (0)1722 716 881 Email: sales@francisfrith.co.uk

See Frith products on the internet at www.francisfrith.com

FREE PRINT OF YOUR CHOICE

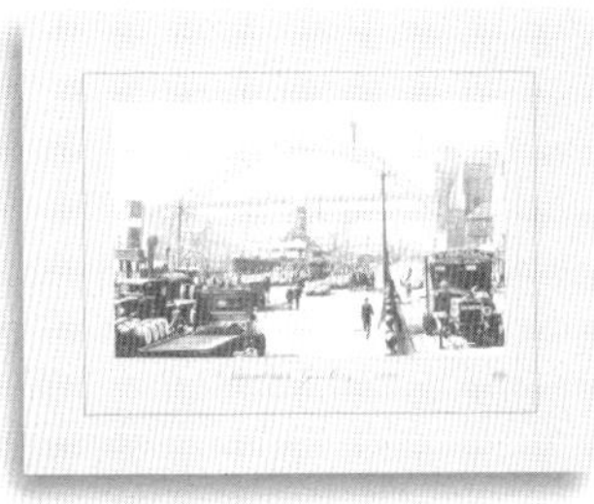

Mounted Print
Overall size 14 x 11 inches (355 x 280mm)

Choose any Frith photograph in this book.
Simply complete the Voucher opposite and return it with your remittance for £3.50 (to cover postage and handling) and we will print the photograph of your choice in SEPIA (size 11 x 8 inches) and supply it in a cream mount with a burgundy rule line (overall size 14 x 11 inches).
Please note: aerial photographs and photographs with a reference number starting with a "Z" are not Frith photographs and cannot be supplied under this offer. Offer valid for delivery to one UK address only.

***PLUS:* Order additional Mounted Prints at HALF PRICE - £9.50 each** (normally £19.00)
If you would like to order more Frith prints from this book, possibly as gifts for friends and family, you can buy them at half price (with no additional postage and handling costs).

***PLUS:* Have your Mounted Prints framed**
For an extra £18.00 per print you can have your mounted print(s) framed in an elegant polished wood and gilt moulding, overall size 16 x 13 inches (no additional postage and handling required).

IMPORTANT!

These special prices are only available if you use this form to order. You must use the ORIGINAL VOUCHER on this page (no copies permitted). We can only despatch to one UK address. This offer cannot be combined with any other offer.

Send completed Voucher form to:
The Francis Frith Collection, Unit 6, Oakley Business Park, Wylye Road, Dinton, Wiltshire SP3 5EU

CHOOSE A PHOTOGRAPH FROM THIS BOOK

Voucher *for **FREE** and Reduced Price Frith Prints*

Please do not photocopy this voucher. Only the original is valid, so please fill it in, cut it out and return it to us with your order.

Picture ref no	Page no	Qty	Mounted @ £9.50	Framed + £18.00	Total Cost £
		1	Free of charge*	£	£
			£9.50	£	£
			£9.50	£	£
			£9.50	£	£
			£9.50	£	£
			£9.50	£	£
			* Post & handling		£3.50
			Total Order Cost		£

Please allow 28 days for delivery.
Offer available to one UK address only

Title of this book ....

I enclose a cheque/postal order for £ ....
made payable to 'The Francis Frith Collection'

OR please debit my Mastercard / Visa / Maestro card, details below

Card Number:

Issue No (Maestro only): Valid from (Maestro):

Card Security Number: Expires:

Signature:

Name Mr/Mrs/Ms ....

Address ....

....

....

.... Postcode ....

Daytime Tel No ....

Email ....

978-1-85937-973-8 Valid to 31/12/12

Free Print - see overleaf

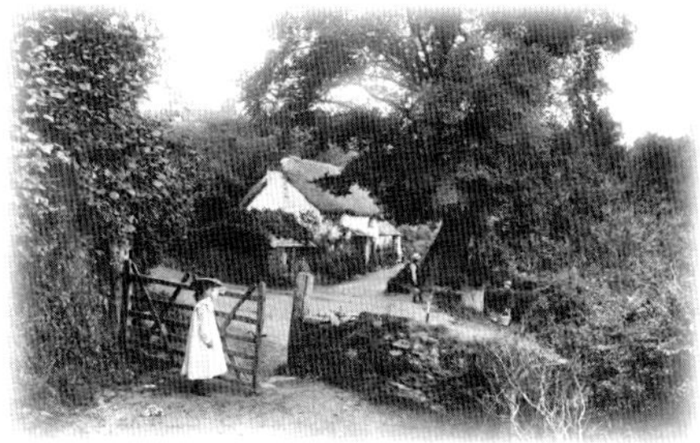

Can you help us with information about any of the Frith photographs in this book?

We are gradually compiling an historical record for each of the photographs in the Frith archive. It is always fascinating to find out the names of the people shown in the pictures, as well as insights into the shops, buildings and other features depicted.

If you recognize anyone in the photographs in this book, or if you have information not already included in the author's caption, do let us know. We would love to hear from you, and will try to publish it in future books or articles.

An Invitation from The Francis Frith Collection to Share Your Memories

The 'Share Your Memories' feature of our website allows members of the public to add personal memories relating to the places featured in our photographs, or comment on others already added. Seeing a place from your past can rekindle forgotten or long held memories. Why not visit the website, find photographs of places you know well and add YOUR story for others to read and enjoy? We would love to hear from you!

www.francisfrith.com/memories

Our production team

Frith books are produced by a small dedicated team at offices near Salisbury. Most have worked with the Frith Collection for many years. All have in common one quality: they have a passion for the Frith Collection.

Frith Books and Gifts

We have a wide range of books and gifts available on our website utilising our photographic archive, many of which can be individually personalised.

www.francisfrith.com